HUNTING FOR
WITCHES

Also by Frances Hill

Nonfiction

A Delusion of Satan: The Full Story of the Salem Witch Trials

Salem: Place, Myth and Memory (contributor)

The Salem Witch Trials Reader

Such Men Are Dangerous: The Fanatics of 1692 and 2004

Fiction

Out of Bounds

A Fatal Delusion

HUNTING FOR
WITCHES

A VISITOR'S GUIDE
TO THE SALEM WITCH TRIALS

FRANCES HILL

COMMONWEALTH EDITIONS
CARLISLE, MASSACHUSETTS

For Tamarin,
who set me hunting in the first place,
with love

Copyright © 2002 by Frances Hill

Library of Congress Cataloging-in-Publication Data

Hill, Frances, 1943–
    Hunting for witches : a visitor's guide to the Salem witch trials / Frances Hill.
        p. cm.
    Includes bibliographical references and index.
    ISBN 978-1-889833-30-4 (pbk.)
        1. Witchcraft--Massachusetts--Salem--History--17th century. 2. Salem (Mass.)--Social conditions. 3. Trials (Witchcraft)--Massachusetts--Salem. I. Title.

BF1576.H54 2002
133.4'3'097445--dc21

2002017368

Book design by Judy Barolak

CE

Commonwealth Editions is an imprint of Applewood Books, Inc.
Box 27, Carlisle, Massachusetts 01741
www.commonwealtheditions.com

Also by Frances Hill

◈

Nonfiction

A Delusion of Satan: The Full Story of the Salem Witch Trials

Salem: Place, Myth and Memory (contributor)

The Salem Witch Trials Reader

Such Men Are Dangerous: The Fanatics of 1692 and 2004

Fiction

Out of Bounds

A Fatal Delusion

HUNTING FOR
WITCHES

January–February 1692
The hysteria is born

Dangerous magic

TWO LITTLE GIRLS were telling their fortunes by the fire on a winter's night in the Salem Village parsonage. They knew they were doing something forbidden. If they were caught, they would incur the Reverend Samuel Parris's terrifying disapproval and wrath. Betty, the pastor's daughter, was nine. Abigail, his niece, who lived with the family, was just two years older. They broke an egg white into a water-filled glass and waited for it to settle into a shape. According to old English folklore this would indicate the profession of the future husband of one of them. The strands of egg white might float to the form of an anchor or a hoe or a Bible. But this time they settled into the shape of a coffin. The girls' guilt and terror were so overwhelming that they went into hysterical fits in which they were "taken dumb, their mouths stopped, their throats choked, their limbs wracked and tormented."[1]

The fits did not stop. Instead, they spread to other girls living nearby. Ann Putnam, age twelve, and Elizabeth Hubbard, age seventeen, soon began exhibiting the same strange behavior. They started "getting into holes, and creeping under chairs and stools, and (using) sturdy odd postures and antic gestures, uttering foolish, ridiculous speeches, which neither they themselves nor any others could make sense of."[2] People whispered that they were bewitched.

A witch cake

IT WAS SOME WEEKS BEFORE such suspicions were confirmed. Dr. William Griggs, a friend and neighbor of Rev. Parris and the uncle and guardian of Elizabeth Hubbard, pronounced the girls "under an evil hand."[3] Parris's Native American slaves, John and Tituba, were induced by another neighbor to bake a "witch cake," containing the girls' urine. The cake was fed to a dog; the belief was that if it died or went into fits that would prove that the girls were bewitched. We do not know what happened to the dog. We do know that Rev. Parris became enraged, claiming that by this action "the devil hath been raised."[4] Parris was a fanatical Puritan with a black-and-white world view and a furious temper. Betty and Abigail began to cry out that Tituba was invisibly pricking and pinching them. They were no doubt responding to the repeated question from Rev. Parris and others, "Who afflicts you?" Soon they were also accusing a beggar, Sarah Good, and a bedridden outcast, Sarah Osborne.

The hysteria: was it genuine or fraudulent?

There can be no doubt that Betty Parris fell into a hysterical fit when she saw what looked like a coffin in the glass. A month later she was removed from Salem Village and the other girls but did not recover. Her fits stopped only later, when she confessed the incident that had started them to a minister. It is less clear whether Abigail Williams, Ann Putnam, and Elizabeth Hubbard were genuinely hysterical or imitating Betty's behavior. There are documented cases throughout history of hysteria being passed from one person to another, sometimes affecting whole communities. It may well be that all the girls' initial fits arose more from the overwhelming desire to let go of psychological restraints than from calculated acting. The first four afflicted girls were soon joined by two others, Mercy Lewis and Mary Walcott, and before long by four more. Their numbers were further increased by a couple of boys, a male Native American slave, and several older women, including Ann Putnam's mother, Thomas's wife, also named Ann.

Many of the women and girls may well have had anxious, troubled characters, predisposed to hysteria. Of the girls, only three lived with both natural parents. The rest were

On February 29, Ann Putnam's father, Thomas Putnam, and his brother Edward, with two other men, traveled to Salem to make a complaint to the magistrates, John Hathorne and Jonathan Corwin. A complaint was an official request for suspects to be arrested and questioned, to see if they ought to be tried. This one stated that Sarah Good, Sarah Osborne, and Tituba had injured Betty Parris, Abigail Williams, Ann Putnam, and Elizabeth Hubbard by witchcraft. The magistrates responded by ordering the three women brought to the village tavern for questioning the next morning at ten. The magistrates' action was not surprising, since the three women—a Native American, a beggar, and an

orphaned or semi-orphaned. The parents of two, Mercy Lewis and Sarah Churchill, had been slaughtered by Indians. The father of another, Susannah Sheldon, was wounded in an Indian attack, later dying of his injuries. Early New England was a dangerous place. The girls, like everyone else, lived in fear of sudden, violent attack from the Indians, of infectious disease, of harsh punishment for minor transgressions, of God's wrath and eternal damnation. Because in the Puritan colonies, pleasures such as singing and dancing were forbidden, this anxiety was combined with a terrible boredom. Anxiety may have started the fits, and boredom may have encouraged the girls to prolong them.

Later, some of the girls practiced trickery and fraud. One of them, Mary Warren, claimed they were all play-acting, though soon after, out of fear, she retracted her statement. Another girl said in an unguarded moment that they were naming people as witches "for sport."[5] Clear evidence of outright deception at the trials can be found in a number of sources. It seems likely that the girls' behavior was a complicated mixture of the involuntary and the voluntary, the innocent and corrupt, varying from one girl to another and one incident to another.

outcast—were already considered misfits in Puritan society, quite likely to be witches.

March 1692
The examinations begin

Evil spirits

WHEN TITUBA, Sarah Good, and Sarah Osborne were brought to Ingersoll's Ordinary, the Salem Village tavern, the crowd wishing to attend their interrogation was so large that the proceedings were moved down the road to the more spacious meetinghouse.

Sarah Good was the first to be interrogated. The transcripts still survive. They were scribbled down in longhand and may not be entirely accurate, but they give us an excellent idea of the questions and answers. The chief magistrate was John Hathorne, the son of a strict Puritan judge who had ordered Quakers to be hanged for following their faith. John inherited his father's merciless beliefs. His first demand was, "Sarah Good, what evil spirit have you familiarity with?" She said, "None." His second question was, "Have you made no contract with the devil?" When she answered, "No," he asked, "Why do you hurt these children?"[6] Not for a moment was there any presumption of innocence. Magistrates in Puritan Massachusetts saw themselves as God's representatives, aiming not to search for the truth but to elicit confessions.

A thing like a man

SARAH GOOD unwaveringly protested her own innocence but was badgered by Hathorne into accusing Sarah Osborne. Sarah Osborne then protested *her* innocence. During both these interrogations, the accusing girls went into fits when the prisoners looked at them. It seems that by now they

The house of magistrate Jonathan Corwin at 310 Essex Street in Salem, the only house remaining in Salem with a direct connection to the witch trials. (Ralph Turcotte photo)

could do this whenever required. When it was Tituba's turn to be examined, the girls began shouting and writhing as she entered the room. But she, too, protested her innocence. Hathorne pressed her relentlessly, ignoring her denials, twisting her words. And at last she succumbed, saying what he and Rev. Parris clearly wanted to hear. She claimed she saw a thing "like a man, I think yesterday, I being in the lean-to chamber, I saw a thing like a man . . ."[7] The "man" was the devil. She confessed to pinching Betty Parris, Abigail Williams, Ann Putnam, and Elizabeth Hubbard, and to riding through the air on a pole with Sarah Osborne and Sarah Good. She kept saying she was sorry, hoping to be saved from imprisonment. The hope was in vain. Together with both Sarahs, she was sent off to jail in Boston.

The net widens

NOW THAT TITUBA had confessed, the way was clear for more daring accusations. The next was of sixty-five-year-old Martha Cory, a respectable member of the Salem Village church and wife of a prosperous farmer and landowner. It is

The Trial of a Witch *by illustrator Howard Pyle, originally published in the article "Giles Cory, Yeoman," in* Harper's *magazine, December 1892.*

more than likely that Thomas Putnam, the father of the accusing girl Ann Putnam, suggested this name. With Rev. Parris, he was to become the leader of the witch hunt. On March 19, Thomas's brother Edward Putnam and his friend Henry Kenney filed a complaint. Martha Cory was examined two days later.

Yellow bird

ON MARCH 20, Martha was subjected to an ordeal almost as harrowing as the examination itself. It was a Sunday, so no warrant could be served and she was free to go to the meetinghouse. The minister was a visiting preacher, Deodat Lawson, invited from Boston by the Putnams. He had been the Salem Village pastor just before Rev. Parris. Now he stood before the congregation and started saying the first prayer. He did not get far, as the group of girls soon began having "sore fits."[8] More had joined the band. By now there were eight of them: Betty Parris, Ann Putnam, Abigail Williams, Elizabeth Hubbard, Mary Walcott (the daughter of a relative of the Putnams), and Mercy Lewis (the Putnams' seventeen-year-old servant), together with two older women, a Mrs. Pope and Goodwife Bibber. The accusers went from "sore fits" to impudence. "Now stand up, and name your text!" Abigail Williams demanded. "Now there is enough of that," Mrs. Pope declared, when Lawson became tedious.

When Lawson started his sermon, Abigail shouted, "Look where Goodwife Cory sits on the beam suckling her yellow bird betwixt her fingers!"[9] Ann Putnam claimed a yellow bird sat on Lawson's hat as it hung on a pin in the pulpit. The congregation must have stared fearfully at Martha Cory, still in her seat, believing she was sending her "specter" and her "familiar" flying around the meetinghouse. A witch's specter, or spirit, which left the witch's body but was under her control, was part of the invisible world everyone believed in. The girls' sighting of specters doing harm, known as "spectral evidence," was to prove crucial in the convictions of alleged witches.

On Monday, Martha Cory was again in the meetinghouse, this time in front of the magistrates. Two more women had joined the accusers. One was "an ancient woman named Goodall," and the other was Ann Putnam's mother.[10] This was the first time, that we know of, that Ann Putnam the mother showed the same mental disorder or propensity for fraud or, more likely, mixture of both, as her daughter. It was not to be the last.

Martha Cory bravely defended herself against Hathorne's vicious questions and the mayhem in the court. The girls screamed, writhed, and mimicked her actions. Mrs. Pope threw her muff and a shoe at her. Martha steadfastly maintained that she was innocent and her accusers were "distracted."[11] But this availed her nothing. She was sent to Salem jail.

A saint is accused

IN THE COURSE of the examination of Martha Cory, Ann Putnam the younger set the scene for the next complaint to be made. She claimed she saw Martha Cory praying to the devil with Rebecca Nurse, a seventy-one-year-old mother and grandmother who was loved and revered as the perfect Puritan woman. But the Putnam family had had bitter disputes over land and other matters with her family for decades. The official complaint to the magistrates came the following Wednesday, from Edward and Jonathan Putnam, Thomas's brother and cousin.

The same day that Martha was examined, the Reverend Deodat Lawson visited Ann Putnam, who was still having fits. After he arrived, she was quiet for a while but then

Part of the transcript of the examination of Martha Cory. (Courtesy, Peabody Essex Museum)

began "to strive violently with her arms and legs" and shout "Goodwife Nurse! Be gone! Be gone!" She shouted at Rebecca Nurse's specter, "The devil will torment your soul, for this your name is blotted out of God's book, and it shall never be put in God's book again . . ."[12]

Several days before at the parsonage, Lawson had been

amazed by Abigail's running into the fireplace and throwing firebrands around the room, claiming Rebecca Nurse was afflicting her. The Putnams seem to have been trying their hardest to recruit him as an ally. They had reason. The populace might well doubt that an irreproachable seventy-year-old matriarch was serving the devil.

One Salem Village family who encouraged such doubts were the Porters, who led the faction in Salem Village politics that opposed the Putnams and their allies. Sometime between March 13, when Ann Putnam first mentioned Rebecca Nurse as a possible witch, and March 23, a group of four villagers led by the patriarch Israel Porter called on Rebecca, lying ill in bed. They wrote an account of the meeting that testified to her goodness and innocence. When they told her she was named as a possible witch, they wrote, "She sat still awhile, being as it were amazed. And then she said, 'Well, as to this thing, I am as innocent as the child unborn. But surely, what sin hath God found out in me unrepented of that he should lay such an affliction upon me in my old age.'"[13]

Later, when Rebecca was in prison, the Porters mounted a petition in her favor signed by thirty-nine people, including eight Putnams. Clearly, the family were not all behind Thomas and Edward on this issue. One Putnam, Joseph, was not behind them on anything. He was Thomas's half-brother. The father of both of them, Thomas Putnam Senior, had had eight children by his first wife and just one, Joseph, by his second. He had left most of his fortune to Joseph, depriving Thomas Junior of his expected inheritance. Joseph had married the daughter of Israel Porter, and his loyalty was all to the Porters.

From sickbed to court

ON MARCH 23, still weak from her illness, Rebecca Nurse was brought from her bed to the meetinghouse. Her exami-

Rebecca Nurse House. (Ralph Turcotte photo)

nation was as frenzied as Martha Cory's. But she too stood firm. Her first words were, "I say before my eternal father I am innocent, and God will clear my innocency."[14] Of her accusers she astutely observed, "I do not think these suffer against their wills."[15] Hathorne said that if the girls were shamming, Rebecca must look on them as murderers since their accusations of witchcraft carried the death penalty. A Puritan fanatic, he lacked the subtlety and insight to see that the pressure on the girls might override their concern for the effects of their actions. Later Rebecca said, "The devil may appear in my shape."[16] This called the girls' evidence into question without impugning their honesty. Some of the colony's most respected ministers were soon to make the same point. But Hathorne would not listen, to Rebecca or to them. He clung to his belief that the devil could not appear to someone in the likeness of any innocent person. Had he considered the possibility and therefore doubted the validity of the girls' spectral evidence, he would have sent the accused home and the witch hunt would have ended. Instead, he sent Rebecca Nurse to prison.

One child is destroyed, another saved

WITH HER WENT ANOTHER ACCUSED who had been examined the same day. Dorcas Good, Sarah Good's daughter, had said little during her own examination, but two days later admitted to keeping a "familiar," a snake. Her mother had given it to her, she said. She was four-and-a-half years old.

The imprisonment of Dorcas Good was among the worst horrors of the witch hunt. Deodat Lawson reported that at her examination, she looked "hale, and well as other children."[17] After being kept in prison for seven or eight months,

---

The motives of Samuel Parris and Thomas Putnam, the chief witch hunters.

The Reverend Samuel Parris was at the center of a bitter Salem Village controversy. Born in London in 1653, he had traveled to the New World as a young man, dropped out of Harvard College, moved to Barbados to run a sugar plantation, failed at that, and gone back to Boston. There, he switched from business to the ministry and, in 1689, moved to Salem Village. His ministry became a pivotal issue in the disputes between factions led by two powerful families, the Putnams and the Porters. Both had been settled in Salem Village for three generations. But the Putnams were exclusively farmers, becoming poorer as they subdivided their land, while the Porters had links with the merchants in Salem Town, becoming more prosperous. The Putnams wanted to bolster their status and power by increasing Salem Village's independence from the town. For this reason, they wanted a Salem Village church with a fully ordained minister. By ruthless maneuvering they forced the Village Committee to give Parris title to the parsonage in 1689. But by 1692, the Porters had gained control of the committee and were threatening to stop the minister's wages. Samuel Parris was terrified that his enemies, led by the Porters, might use what was happening against him, claiming that his daughter and niece were witches

---

chained to a wall, she did not look at all hale. She had gone mad. Having "little or no reason to govern herself,"[18] as her father described it, she had to be cared for by a keeper for the rest of her life. It is hard to see what motive Thomas Putnam could have had for targeting a four-year-old. It is possible that the girls themselves may have done it, out of sheer malice.

By contrast, another young player in this drama, Betty Parris, was sent to stay with a family in Salem, away from the other girls. She took no further part in the witch hunt. The

themselves. He beat Tituba to try to make her confess that she was the witch. Soon Parris and his allies, the Putnams, realized they had been handed a formidable weapon in the guise of witch-finding relatives. With skillful management, the young people could "cry out on" anyone their parents and guardians chose. It is likely that Parris saw this strategy as a way of safeguarding his reputation and livelihood.

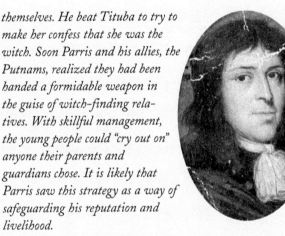

The Reverend Samuel Parris. (Massachusetts Historical Society)

Thomas Putnam, the father of Ann Putnam, was angry, and envious of the prosperity, relative freedom, and tolerance of Salem Town merchants and their allies. He was ready to use any means to lash out at them, as well as at enemies nearer home. Though his targeting of victims was often carefully calculated, it was also often impulsive, driven by irrational hatred rather than expectation of material gain. During the witch hunt at least one Putnam family member signed fifteen of the twenty-one recorded complaints that survive.

best view of this is that her parents loved her enough to want to avoid harming her by prolonging her fits. A less benign possibility is that the Putnams wanted only performers fully aware of their actions. Betty was genuinely ill and may never have been party to fraud.

A door slams

ON SUNDAY, MARCH 27, Rev. Parris was back in the pulpit that had been lent a week before to Deodat Lawson. He used the opportunity to justify Rebecca Nurse's arrest, delivering a sermon entitled, "Christ knows how many devils there are in his churches, and who they are." When he named as his text "One of you is a devil," Rebecca's sister, Sarah Cloyce, marched out of the meetinghouse, slamming the door. Like everyone else, she knew the sermon was aimed at her sister. Later the accusers claimed to see Sarah in a field outside the parsonage window, holding a devilish sacrament with forty other witches. A week later, a complaint was made against her, together with Elizabeth Proctor, another respectable church member, by Thomas Putnam's allies Jonathan Walcott, the father of Mary, and Nathaniel Ingersoll.

April 1692
The witch hunt expands

The first man is accused

UP TO THIS POINT, the unfolding drama had taken place in Salem Village. The main players had come from there or Salem Town. Now the leaders of Massachusetts Bay Colony began to take an interest. Their concern arose partly from the sheer number of accusations. In the more than fifty years since the Puritans had founded the colony, witchcraft accusations had focused on one or two people at a time. In April

House built on the site of John Proctor's home in present-day Peabody. (Ralph Turcotte photo)

1692, there were six alleged witches in jail. That, and the alleged sighting by Abigail Williams of a large group of devil worshippers taking their sacrament, suggested more than commonplace witchcraft. Leading ministers had been warning for years of a conspiracy, headed by the devil, to conquer Massachusetts. It now seemed this was happening.

A second cause of the widening interest was that a man was among the accused. A male witch suspect was always seen as a possible leader. This man was John Proctor, Elizabeth's husband, named by Abigail Williams as tormenting her, though not yet complained of. It is no surprise that the Putnams might have accused him. When his maid, Mary Warren, joined the accusers, he threatened to "thrash the devil out of her" and cried of the afflicted girls, in front of a witness, "Hang them! Hang them!"[19] Such a man was clearly a threat, if not as a leader of witches, then as a leader of skeptics.

On April 11, with several top Boston ministers, no less a figure than Thomas Danforth, deputy governor of the colony, presided at Salem meetinghouse in Salem Town.

Leading questions

Danforth started by addressing John Indian, Parris's slave and the husband of Tituba. John was now one of the accusers. After seeing his wife thrown into jail, he must have decided that he would rather accuse than be accused. Danforth asked him who had hurt him. He named Goody Cloyce and Goody Proctor. The examination proceeded with Danforth asking questions that presupposed knowledge of the answers, such as, "Abigail Williams! Did you see a company at Mr. Parris's house eat and drink?" and "Mary Walcott, have you seen a white man?"[20] The girls started going into fits, and the examination became as chaotic as those in Salem Village.

"By and by," Samuel Parris narrates in his account, "both of them [Abigail Williams and Ann Putnam] cried out of Goodman Proctor himself, and said he was a wizard. Immediately, many, if not all of the bewitched, had grievous fits."[21] In due course, John, his wife, and Sarah Cloyce were committed to prison.

A spate of accusations

NOW THAT THE WITCH HUNT had been given the seal of approval from Boston, the complaints came in droves. John Hathorne was kept busy through April in the Salem Village meetinghouse, examining people the Putnams hated, envied, or feared. These included Giles Cory, who had initially given evidence against his wife Martha but now opposed the witch hunt; Bridget Bishop, who was rumored to have been a witch for several decades; Abigail Hobbs, a wild young woman of Topsfield who roamed the woods at night by herself; Mary Easty, the sister of Rebecca Nurse and Sarah Cloyce; and seventeen others. Every complaint bore the name Putnam, either Thomas or John. The month climaxed with the most ambitious shot yet, against a man of considerable talent and standing, the Reverend George Burroughs.

Reconstruction of the Salem Village meetinghouse, on the grounds of the Rebecca Nurse homestead. (Ralph Turcotte photo)

A little black minister

BURROUGHS WAS ANOTHER former Salem Village minister, but unlike Deodat Lawson he was no Putnam ally. A Harvard College graduate, of famed bravery and strength, so short and dark he was once referred to as "a little black minister," he had preached in the distant Maine settlement of Casco under constant threat of attack by Indians.[22] When that attack came in 1676, he escaped to Salisbury, Massachusetts and, four years later, came to Salem Village. He was a free spirit willing to preach to dissenters, and his approach to life and religion was the opposite of the Putnams'. The particular disagreements between Rev. Burroughs and that family are obscure, but the finale is well documented. During it, the Putnams were humiliated. Then in 1683, Rev. Burroughs left Salem Village to return to Casco.

Nine years later, the time came for the Putnams' revenge. At her examination in late April, Deliverance Hobbs, mother of Abigail, claimed that she had seen Burroughs acting as minister at a witches' parody of a sacrament. She overheard him urging his followers to bewitch the whole village. Presumably Deliverance was handpicked for such accusations because she had lived in Maine with her husband and daughter and knew Burroughs.

The next development was a letter from Thomas Putnam to John Hathorne and Jonathan Corwin, intended to soften them up for almost incredible news. "Much honoured," it begins, its tone fawning but insidious. "After most humble and hearty thanks presented to your Honours for the great care and pains you have already taken for us . . . , we . . . thought it our duty to inform your Honours of what we conceive you have not heard, which are high and dreadful; of a wheel within a wheel, at which our ears do tingle." It ends with the hope "that you may be a terror to evil-doers and a praise to them that do well."[23]

No doubt, after sending this, Thomas Putnam followed his letter with a visit to the magistrates in person. The "high and dreadful" matters were almost certainly his daughter Ann's visions of Rev. Burroughs. According to testimony handed in later, Burroughs's specter had told Ann, on the day before Putnam wrote his letter, that he had killed his first two wives by witchcraft. He had done the same to Deodat Lawson's wife and child and many soldiers in Maine. He claimed that he had also made Abigail Hobbs and several other people witches. And he said of himself that he was "above a witch for he was a conjurer."[24]

Two weeks later, a few days before Burroughs's examination, Ann saw the dead wives themselves, or so her father claimed. The wives told her Burroughs had murdered them, one saying he had stabbed her under the arm. She pulled aside her winding sheet, showing Ann the wound.

Thomas Putnam's painstaking maneuvers duly led to a marshal being sent the considerable distance to Casco to escort Burroughs back to Salem. It is no surprise that Hathorne played a part in arranging this. He had his own reasons for wishing Burroughs dead. The second of the wives George Burroughs was supposed to have murdered had been Hathorne's brother's widow. She came from a wealthy Salem family that had opposed her making a match with an obscure village minister. Her family and the Hathornes were close. John Hathorne may have abhorred the murder of a relative, but he may equally have resented the penniless Burroughs's winning that relative's hand in the first place.

Enemies in high places

THERE WAS ANOTHER, more telling reason why Hathorne, and others more powerful than he was, disliked Burroughs. The minister was by no means an orthodox Puritan. In Maine, a region only tenuously under Puritan control, he preached to Anglicans and Baptists. He had not taken communion for years and had failed to have most of his children baptized. The Puritan hierarchy was terrified of this sort of laxity, amounting to dissent.

Their fear is clearly shown by the fact that Rev. Burroughs's examination took place in Salem, conducted by two of the most powerful men in the colony. William Stoughton was about to replace Danforth as deputy governor, under the new charter, while the Reverend Samuel Sewall was a leading minister and judge. Also present, as always, were Hathorne and Corwin.

The interrogators began by asking Burroughs about his religious observances. They could do so in peace since the accusing girls were kept out of the room. They asked when he had last taken communion. Burroughs said it had been so long before that he could not remember. He admitted he had been to services where communion was served and had failed to take it. The questioners then asked if the house he lived in was haunted. He denied it but "owned there were toads."[25] Toads in Puritan eyes were sinister creatures, perhaps minions of Satan. Next, Burroughs was forced to admit that none of his children but the eldest was baptized. This was his most damning admission so far because baptism had become a highly charged issue in the Puritan church. Baptists, who rejected the baptism of infants, were loathed and despised as much as Anglicans and even Catholics. Burroughs had thus condemned himself before he even faced his accusers.

When they were let in the room, the accusers went through all the expected motions, screaming, writhing, and

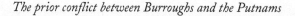

The prior conflict between Burroughs and the Putnams

When the Reverend George Burroughs first arrived in Salem Village, in 1680, the parsonage needed repairs, and he and his wife stayed with John Putnam Senior, Thomas's uncle, and his wife. There was friction between the two couples, but after nine months the parsonage was ready and the Burroughses moved in. A year later, Mrs. Burroughs died. Burroughs borrowed money from John Putnam to pay her funeral expenses. In 1683, the Village Committee stopped paying his salary due to the frictions between him and the Putnams, and he went back to Casco. On May 2, he returned for a meeting to settle his debts. The expectation was that the Village would pay his back salary and he would pay what he owed. Instead, John Putnam had the minister arrested. Everyone present was astonished. Even Nathaniel Ingersoll protested. But John and his brother Thomas insisted that the marshall take Burroughs to Ingersoll's tavern and "secure him till the morning."[26]

Six villagers came forward to post bail for Burroughs, and at Salem County Court on June 26, 1683, after Burroughs's salary was paid and the outstanding debts settled, John Putnam dropped his charges. Burroughs went back to Casco, no doubt thinking he would never see Salem Village again. He did not anticipate the Putnams' furious vindictiveness.

falling down when Burroughs looked at them. Ann Putnam and a newcomer, Susannah Sheldon, claimed to see his dead wives. The mother-and-daughter team who had once lived in Maine, Deliverance and Abigail Hobbs, said they had been at the witches' meeting in the pasture next to Rev. Parris's house, where Burroughs had administered the sacrament. Witnesses were brought forward to testify to his superhuman strength, thought to come only from the devil, and his cruelty to his wives. He was committed to jail. His hanging was to be one of the most dramatic and moving of the nineteen in Salem. But that would be several months later.

May 1692
The rich and famous are targeted

Intolerance and envy

BY MAY, the pace of the witch hunt had become ever faster and more furious. The girls no longer confined their accusations to Salem Village or people they knew. They began targeting such luminaries as Phillip English, the richest merchant in Salem.

English's wealth might have been reason enough for the Putnams to loathe him. He owned fourteen town lots, a wharf, more than twenty sailing ships, and a splendid house. But there were other reasons, too. In April, following a failed attempt by the Putnams to make a comeback in town politics, English and his ally Daniel Andrew had been elected as Salem Town selectmen. What was more, English was an Anglican. In 1733, he would give a piece of Salem Town land on which to build an Anglican church.

Phillip and his wife, also named, avoided arrest and, when later caught, escaped from jail. No one wealthy stayed in jail for long since jailers were corruptible. Daniel Andrew was also targeted and also evaded arrest.

Ordeals and escapes

OTHER LOFTY TARGETS were Elizabeth Cary, the wife of Nathaniel Cary, a wealthy Charlestown merchant, and John Alden, a well-known Boston mariner, the son of the John Alden who had founded Plymouth Colony. They were both arrested and imprisoned but escaped. Nathaniel Cary's account of what happened tells us much about the methods of the witch hunters. When he heard his wife was accused, he says, they went to Salem Village. There was an examination in progress. Two girls of about ten years old, and two or three of about eighteen, were having fits as the prisoners were brought in. When one of the girls touched a prisoner, the magistrate pronounced that she was cured of her fits, before he had seen any actual change. The girls took no notice of Nathaniel's wife except to ask her her name.

Nathaniel Cary asked Beverly's minister John Hale, who was present, to arrange for his wife to speak privately with

The magistrates' and ministers' agendas

The Massachusetts Bay Colony was ruled by an elite composed mainly of descendants of the original settlers. Many were both ministers and elected politicians. By 1692, they felt increasingly threatened by the pressure for greater religious tolerance and freedom, both from within Massachusetts and from England. Modern scientific ideas were at last reaching Massachusetts. Two leading ministers, Increase and Cotton Mather, father and son, both wrote books about witchcraft and other "remarkable occurrences" to bolster fears of supernatural phenomena. The Salem Village witch hunt may have seemed to them, literally, a godsend.

The Massachusetts leaders' anxiety was heightened by threats to their regime from without. In 1684, the charter from England that guaranteed the right to enforce Puritanism as the

her accuser, Abigail Williams. Reverend Hale agreed to this, but then, after sending the Carys to Ingersoll's tavern, loosed all the girls on them. The girls fell on the ground and shouted that Elizabeth Cary was bewitching them. Elizabeth was taken straight to the magistrates, who seemed to be expecting her. She asked Nathaniel to wipe the tears from her eyes and the sweat from her face, which he did, and then asked if she could lean on him, saying she might faint. Hathorne declared that since she had strength enough to torture the accusers she should have strength enough to stand. Nathaniel protested at this cruelty and was told to be quiet or be thrown out of the room.

Elizabeth was ordered to prison. Nathaniel managed to have her taken to the local jail in Cambridge instead of the one in Boston, but after one night there the jailer put irons on her legs. This sent her into convulsions, and her husband was afraid she would die. He went to view the trials in Salem

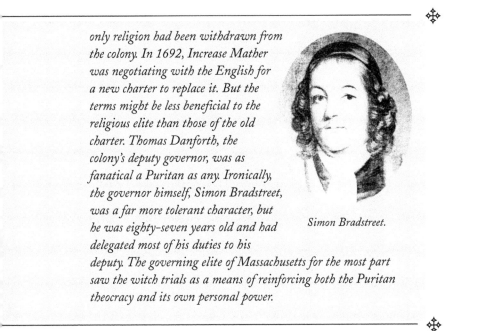

only religion had been withdrawn from the colony. In 1692, Increase Mather was negotiating with the English for a new charter to replace it. But the terms might be less beneficial to the religious elite than those of the old charter. Thomas Danforth, the colony's deputy governor, was as fanatical a Puritan as any. Ironically, the governor himself, Simon Bradstreet, was a far more tolerant character, but he was eighty-seven years old and had delegated most of his duties to his deputy. The governing elite of Massachusetts for the most part saw the witch trials as a means of reinforcing both the Puritan theocracy and its own personal power.

Simon Bradstreet.

to see if there was any hope of justice, concluded that there was not, and helped his wife to escape. They went to the colony of New York, where, with other escapees, they were received courteously by the governor. Nathaniel and Elizabeth were eventually able to return home to Charlestown and take up their lives again. Theirs is one of the few stories about an accused witch that had a happy ending.

John Alden also left a graphic account of his travail. He was sent for by the magistrates after being accused by what he calls "a company of poor, distracted, or possessed creatures or witches . . . who played their juggling tricks, falling down, crying out, and staring in peoples' faces."[27] When he touched them, they said the touch made them well again. Alden was jailed but was also rich and influential enough to escape eventually from prison and continue with his life.

Margaret Jacobs's retraction of her confession

In her recantation, Margaret wrote, ". . . your poor and humble declarant being confined here in Salem gaol for the crime of witchcraft, which crime thanks be to the Lord I am altogether ignorant of, as will appear at the great day of judgment: may it please the honoured court, I was cried out upon by some of the possessed persons, as afflicting them; whereupon I was brought to my examination, which persons at the sight of me fell down, which did very much startle and affright me. The Lord above knows I knew nothing, in the least measure, how or who afflicted them; they told me, if I would not confess, I should be put down into the dungeon and would be hanged, but if I would confess I should have my life; the which did so affright me, with my own vile wicked heart, to save my life; made me make the like confession I did, which confession, may it please the honoured court, is altogether false and untrue. The very first night after I had made confession, I was in such horror of conscience that I could not sleep for fear the devil should carry me away for telling such horrid

---

Lowlier targets

LESS FORTUNATE, because poorer and humbler, was George Jacobs, an eighty-year-old farmer. One cause for his being targeted was that he was Daniel Andrew's relative by marriage, as was true of his sixteen-year-old granddaughter, Margaret. Their stories are notable because of the extraordinary bravery they showed. George, so crippled by arthritis that he walked with two sticks, made the declaration that would later become famous, "Burn me or hang me, I will stand in the truth of Christ."[28]

Margaret Jacobs, threatened with the gallows, made a confession and named her grandfather and George Burroughs as witches, but then she retracted it. Her retraction, excerpted on pages 38 and 39, which she knew might bring about her death, tells us a great deal about the methods of the witch

---

lies. . . . What I said, was altogether false against my grandfather [George Jacobs], and Mr. Burroughs, which I did to save my life and to have my liberty; but the Lord, charging it to my conscience, made me in so much horror, that I could not contain myself before I had denied my confession, which I did though I saw nothing but death before me, choosing rather death with a quiet conscience, than to live in such horror, which I could not suffer. Where, upon my denying my confession, I was committed to close prison, where I have enjoyed more felicity in spirit, a thousand times, than I did before in my enlargement."[29]

The night before George Burroughs's execution Margaret Jacobs asked his forgiveness for testifying against him, and he both forgave her and prayed with her. As a result of recanting, she was thrown into a dungeon instead of being allowed the relative freedom and ease of the upper floor of the prison. Luckily, she was not tried in the Court of Oyer and Terminer, due to illness. In January 1693, she was tried and acquitted in the Superior Court.

---

hunters as well as about her. Especially worth noting is that the magistrates explicitly informed her that if she confessed she would live.

The witch court

IN THE MIDDLE of this hectic month of complaints and arrests, the new governor of Massachusetts arrived from England with the long-awaited charter. A self-made man, knighted by King William after finding sunken treasure, Sir William Phips was baffled by the "horrible witchcraft."[30] He turned for advice to William Stoughton, the new deputy governor, who advised him to set up a special court to try the accused witches. Phips did so, appointing Stoughton its chief judge. Then Governor Phips promptly left for the outlying areas of Maine to fight the Indians and the French.

The Court of Oyer and Terminer, which would sit in the Town House in Salem, at once began preparations for the first of its trials. The suspect was chosen with care. Of all the accused witches, Bridget Bishop would be the safest to con-

An old print showing royal governor Sir William Phips landing in Boston from England on May 14, 1692.

William Stoughton.

Cotton Mather. (Courtesy, Peabody Essex Museum)

vict and the least controversial because she had a long history of accusations against her. The prosecution would not have to rely on the accusing girls' spectral evidence but could bring forward a range of deponents to tell stories of her witchcraft.

The issue of spectral evidence had been causing increasing unease. On May 31, the Boston minister Cotton Mather, son of Increase, had written a letter to one of the judges of the court, warning that "it is very certain that the devils have sometimes represented the shapes of persons not only innocent but also very virtuous."[31] Cotton Mather's dedication to rooting out witches and to fostering supernatural beliefs was extreme, so the fact that, of anyone, he should issue this warning shows how widespread the doubts really were.

June 1692
The first trial and hanging

Poppets of hogs' bristles and rags

BECAUSE OF THESE DOUBTS about spectral evidence, much was made at Bridget's trial of the nearest approximation to hard evidence that the court could bring against her. On June

Bridget Bishop's death warrant, June 10, 1692. (Courtesy, Peabody Essex Museum)

2, before the bench of seven judges, the band of accusers, deponents, and spectators, she was accused of owning dolls used for witchcraft. Several "poppets made up of rags and hogs' bristles with headless pins in them." had been found in the holes of the cellar wall of a house she had lived in, according to the father and son who had demolished it.[32] Since Bridget had no defense lawyer, there was no one to suggest that there might be an innocent explanation for the presence of the objects, or that they might have been planted, or that the men might be lying.

There also was no one to argue against the existence of a "preternatural teat" supposedly found on Bridget's body "between the pudendum and anus" by a doctor and nine illiterate women.[33] There was no one to suggest it might be a pimple, mole, or some other growth, or perhaps a dropped womb. And there was no one to challenge the long troop of witnesses who claimed Bridget had caused harm to them by witchcraft, though many years later one of these witnesses admitted, on his deathbed, that he had lied.

The accusing girls screamed, choked, and writhed at the trial as they had at the examinations. One girl claimed Bridget's shape had taken her from her spinning wheel, carried her to the river, and threatened to drown her. Another said her specter had bragged that she "had been the death of sundry persons." She also claimed that apparitions had appeared in the court and cried out to Bishop, "You murdered us!"[34] The "harm" Bridget had done at the examination was used as evidence now, as was the harm supposedly done at the trial. Her death warrant states that she was found guilty of "witchcraft in and upon the bodies of Abigail Williams, Ann Putnam Junior, Mercy Lewis, Mary Walcott and Elizabeth Hubbard," attesting that spectral evidence remained central despite all efforts to downplay it.[35]

The hanging tree

ON JUNE 10, at eight o'clock in the morning, Bridget Bishop was carried on a cart from Salem Jail near North River, along Prison Lane to Essex Street, and then to the Boston Road and a tall, rocky hill. On the way, an incident took place that

Part of Gallows Hill today. (Ralph Turcotte photo)

Cotton Mather regarded as extra proof of her witchcraft. According to his account in *Wonders of the Invisible World,* as her cart passed the Salem meetinghouse, Bridget looked toward the building, causing a board to break loose from its nails and fly across the room. Presumably what really occurred was that by coincidence a board came away from the wall as Bridget was passing. What happened to it afterwards was no doubt embellished with each retelling of the story.

Either from the branch of a tree or a newly made gallows, surrounded by spectators, Bridget breathed her last. One judge was so dissatisfied with the proceedings that he resigned from the bench. He was Nathaniel Saltonstall of Haverhill. In due course, the girls would cry out against *him.* Saltonstall was not alone in his concerns. Governor Phips was troubled enough to ask the advice of several Boston ministers on how the court should proceed. Their response was an unhelpful piece of prose entitled *Return of the Several Ministers Consulted.* Probably penned by Cotton Mather, it advised caution about the use of spectral evidence while urging the speedy, vigorous prosecution of witches. It declined to suggest how witches could be prosecuted, speedily or otherwise, without using spectral evidence. This is not surprising, since they couldn't be. Cotton Mather wanted to appear cautious, wise, and fair but at the same time to encourage the witch hunt.

The witch hunt moves to Andover

DESPITE OR BECAUSE OF this small masterpiece of doublethink, the next months were the busiest yet for the magistrates, judges, and accusers. The outlying town of Andover generated its own, partly independent persecution, with its own band of accusers, in due course sending more accused people to jail than anywhere else, even Salem Village. But Andover's witch hunt began only after one of its residents was targeted by the Salem Village band. Martha Carrier was an independent, outspoken woman, the victim of several previous witchcraft accusations. She was also the sister-in-law of a man who had been arrested for witchcraft two weeks before. Ann Putnam and the rest seem to have targeted him for rivaling them as a witch finder. He was a doctor who claimed to catch witches by heating their urine in a pot in the oven. He said he had taught his daughter this method. She had put the urine to heat overnight, and in the morning the witch suspect was found dead.

The accusers may have targeted Martha Carrier because she was this doctor's relative and a likely witch suspect. She was already highly unpopular because residents suspected her of having brought smallpox to Andover. She was also a relative by marriage of the Andover minister, Francis Dane, who had expressed doubts about the witch hunt. At her examination Martha said, "It is a shameful thing that you should mind these folks that are out of their wits."[36] Cotton Mather later labelled her "Queen of Hell."[37]

There were two factions in Andover as there were in

Salem Village, one representing the rigid values of the past, fearful of change, the other more forward-looking. The first was associated with the new minister Thomas Barnard, brought in to replace the old minister, Francis Dane. The more progressive faction was led by Rev. Dane himself, who refused to retire. Thomas Barnard was a close friend of Cotton Mather and soon became an active promoter of the witch hunt. Dane opposed the accusations and arrests. In due course, about ten of Rev. Dane's close relatives were imprisoned for witchcraft, including two of his daughters and four of his grandchildren. The Andover factions differed from those of Salem Village in that the original settlers were not allies of the persecuting minister. Many became witch-hunt targets themselves, for the sake of their assets and land, which were seized on their convictions by the sheriff.

After Martha Carrier's imprisonment there was a lull in the Andover witch hunt. However, the constable who had taken Martha to her examination in Salem Village and returned to tell of the proceedings of the court and fits of the girls, had a brother with an ailing wife he believed was bewitched. That brother invited Mary Walcott and Ann Putnam to discover who had bewitched her. Soon after the girls' visit in mid-July and their accusation of the elderly Ann Foster, a group of Andover girls began going into fits and making accusations.

Last Salem Village arrests
MEANWHILE, IN SALEM VILLAGE, the numbers examined first increased but then by the end of June dwindled. The last person arrested there, on July 1, was a black slave named Candy. The accusers at her examination were second-string performers such as Mary Warren and the Hobbses, since Ann Putnam, Abigail Williams, Mercy Lewis, and Elizabeth Hubbard had by this time far more important tasks to attend

to. On June 29, and for several days after, they starred at the Court of Oyer and Terminer trials of Sarah Good, Rebecca Nurse, Susannah Martin, Elizabeth Howe, and Sarah Wildes. On July 19 they accompanied the five women to Gallows Hill to their deaths.

Rebecca Nurse's trial

AT THE JUNE 29 TRIALS, despite the troops of deponents brought forward to testify to the accused women's alleged witchcraft, the main evidence was spectral.

Rebecca Nurse's trial was the strangest. To the judges' surprise, if no one else's, the jury found the revered, elderly woman not guilty. After a momentary silence, the accusers went wild. They must have excelled themselves since everyone was astonished by their "hideous outcry."[38] Soon a crowd of disturbed souls outside the court seized the chance of licensed hysteria by joining the afflicted and adding to the clamor. One judge said he was dissatisfied; another, walking off the bench, threatened to have Rebecca retried. William Stoughton declared that he had no wish to impose on the jury but wondered if they had sufficiently considered the remark Rebecca had made when Deliverance Hobbs and her daughter Abigail had been brought in to give evidence. Rebecca had turned her head and exclaimed, "What, do you bring her? She is one of us."[39] What Rebecca meant, Stoughton suggested, was "one of us witches."

The jury went out again. This time they could not agree on their verdict and returned to question the prisoner. The foreman, Thomas Fisk, walked up to her where she stood at the bar and asked what she had meant by her words. She did not reply. He assumed that she could not find a satisfactory answer, and the jury changed its verdict. She was sentenced to hang. Later she wrote a declaration to the court explaining what had occurred.

"I intended no otherways, than as they were prisoners with

us," she said, explaining that she therefore believed them not qualified to give evidence. "And I being something hard of hearing, and full of grief,"[40] she continued, had not realized how the court had interpreted her words and had had no opportunity to explain what she meant.

It is clear that when Fisk had asked her his question she had been so overwhelmed by anxiety and distress that she neither saw nor heard him. Her declaration was ignored. That same afternoon she was excommunicated from Salem Town church.

July 1692
Five more are put to death

Dismal outcries

A FURTHER BITTER TWIST was to take place before Rebecca was executed. Governor Phips granted her a reprieve. Presumably he was persuaded to do so by some of those who had signed the petition in her favor, saying they had never

---

The Jurors

The juries for the Court of Oyer and Terminer were made up of male householders who were members of a church. In other words, they were drawn from the segment of the population which, under the old charter, had the vote. This excluded women, adult males living with their parents, and those who were not church members, comprising not only indigents, indentured servants, and slaves but also respectable Puritans who had not gone through the lengthy procedure necessary to be admitted into a church. Being a member of a church meant having the right to take the sacraments. More fundamentally, it meant being one of God's elect with the expectation of going to heaven. Given the composition of the juries, it is no surprise that they followed the

---

had grounds to suspect her of witchcraft. However, the afflicted girls immediately "renewed their dismal outcries against her," and Phips was prevailed on by "some Salem gentlemen" to rescind it.[41] No doubt these included John Hathorne, Jonathan Corwin, and Bartholomew Gedney. Rebecca was hanged with the four others tried and convicted, on the same raised ground where Bridget Bishop had perished.

These hangings upped the stakes. The skeptics now had an even more serious cause, and thus the witch hunters had greater reason to fear them. The executions offered a spectacle at which the crowd could be swayed to stronger or weaker belief in the guilt of the accused. Desperate to maintain their credibility, the girls mocked the prisoners as they waited to be hanged. So did the Salem minister Nicholas Noyes, a fanatical Puritan who had helped drive on the witch hunt from the start. But the accusers and ministers had powerful forces of goodness, courage, and spirit to contend with. Rebecca Nurse, allowed to speak her last words from the ladder that leaned against the gallows, displayed Christian for-

❖

judges' lead in finding all the accused witches guilty. As ultraconventional Puritans, they were likely to defer to William Stoughton, deputy governor of the colony as well as chief judge. In only one case, that of Rebecca Nurse, did they bring in a verdict of not guilty, which they were then pressured to reverse by the outcries of the afflicted and Stoughton's order to reconsider.

The juries for the Superior Court, which would be set up in December to replace the Court of Oyer and Terminer, were drawn from a broader segment of the population. The new charter had come into effect, and under its rules all male householders, whether church members or not, could serve on a jury. This is one reason why only three of the twenty-four accused witches brought to trial before the Superior Court were convicted. The other was that spectral evidence was no longer admissable.

❖

giveness and humility though inisisting on her innocence. So did Elizabeth Howe and Sarah Wildes, who were also pious, respectable church members. Susannah Martin, who had shown herself clever and bold at her examination, may have made disquieting remarks now. When Nicholas Noyes said she was a witch, the pipe-smoking beggar Sarah Good told him he was a liar, declaring, "I am no more a witch than you are a wizard, and if you take away my life, God will give you blood to drink."[42] By coincidence, presumably, Noyes later died of a brain hemorrhage that made his mouth run with blood.

August 1692
A need for witnesses

Burroughs no likely witch

THE MERE FACT that five convicted witches had refused to confess to their witchcraft, even on the gallows, gave the witch hunters cause for alarm. The next trial was to take place on August 5, and among those to be called to the bar were four men including the Reverend George Burroughs, the former minister of Salem Village. Anyone with doubts about the witch hunt would be even less likely to believe he was a witch than Rebecca Nurse or Elizabeth Howe. The men driving on the madness—Cotton Mather, William Stoughton, John Hathorne, George and Jonathan Corwin, Nicholas Noyes, John Hale, Samuel Parris, and Thomas Putnam and his brothers—badly needed to convince the population that Satan was trying to conquer New England, was signing up witches in droves, and was using Burroughs as their leader. More than anything, they needed accused prisoners who would testify that they or their specters had seen Burroughs in action.

Forced confessions

SO FAR, THERE WERE only five confessors: Tituba, Abigail and Deliverance Hobbs, Margaret Jacobs (who later recanted), and Candy, a black slave. Samuel Parris, Nicholas Noyes, and John Hale had all visited prisoners to try to make them confess, with little success. But on the day of George Burroughs's trial, Cotton Mather sent a letter to his grandfather, John Cotton, crowing triumphantly that God had produced five witches in Andover who had made extraordinary confessions and had agreed Burroughs was their ringleader.

How had this happened? It may be that the Reverend Thomas Barnard of Andover was more adept at persuading people to confess than were ministers Parris, Noyes, and Hale. Of course these people, unlike those jailed earlier, had seen six witches hanged. Yet people jailed earlier could have changed their stories now. Perhaps a significant new factor was that the prisoners were being subjected to pressure

---

Outright deception

    At the start of the witch hunt, the accusing girls may have been genuinely hysterical, but by the time of the trials they were practicing trickery and fraud.

    When Sarah Good stood at the bar, one of the accusers cried out that Sarah had stabbed her in the breast with a knife. The girl produced part of a blade. But a young man claimed it as his, saying he had broken it the day before, when she was near him. He showed the court the rest of the knife, which the blade fitted perfectly. The girl was reproved for telling lies but allowed to continue giving evidence. At Rebecca Nurse's trial Sarah, Rebecca's adult daughter, saw Goodwife Bibber pull pins out of her clothes, stick them in her knees, and cry out that Goody Nurse had pricked her. At Bridget Bishop's trial the accusing girls pointed to her torn coat and said the tear was in a place where Jonathan Walcott had struck at her specter. Despite these transparent deceptions, the trials continued.

Andover house built for the Reverend Thomas Barnard in 1711. (Ralph Turcotte photo)

amounting to torture. It is at this stage that we hear of "tying neck and heels," sleep deprivation, and noise torture. This last seems to have consisted of continuous loud, discordant sounds that the prisoners could not escape. "Tying neck and heels" was an English method of restraint, in which the body was bent double so a rope could tie the neck to the ankles.

John Proctor's plea

ON JULY 23, John Proctor wrote a letter from Salem prison to Increase Mather and four other Boston ministers, whom he had good reason to regard as fairer minded than Cotton, begging for assistance since "our accusers and our judges and jury [have] condemned us already before our trials . . ." He went on, "Here are five persons who have lately confessed themselves to be witches, and do accuse some of us, of being along with them at a sacrament . . . which we knew to be lies. Two of the five are . . . young men, who would not confess anything till they had tied them neck and heels till the blood was ready to come out of their noses."[43] The two young men were the sons of Martha Carrier. After being tied till their noses bled, they accused not only John Proctor but also their own mother.

All the confessors told the same stories about riding to witch meetings on poles, taking part in devilish sacraments administered by George Burroughs, and signing the devil's book with their blood. This was tame stuff compared with confessions made in Europe about wild orgies and the killing and eating of babies. But it was good enough for Cotton Mather. In fact, it was exactly what he wanted. The prisoners, exhausted by sleep deprivation and being forced to stand upright for hours, were asked by the ministers and magistrates, "Were you at such a witch meeting, or have you signed the devil's book?"[44] When they finally said yes, the stories were written up and the prisoners made to sign them as confessions.

Hellish rendezvous

THUS THE GROUND WAS PREPARED for the next set of trials and hangings. On August 5, John and Elizabeth Proctor, strong-minded Martha Carrier, eighty-year-old George Jacobs, a Salem Villager named John Willard, and the Reverend George Burroughs were escorted from Salem prison to the Town House. From Cotton Mather's viewpoint, all of their trials went amazingly well, especially Burroughs's. No fewer than eight "confessing witches" claimed that he was the "head actor at some of their hellish rendezvous" and "nine persons" bore witness to his "extraordinary lifting and such feats of strength as could not be done without a diabolical assistance."[45] Increase Mather, more truly concerned than his son about the use of spectral evidence, was so impressed by this nonspectral testimony that he said, had he been a juryman, he would have found Burroughs guilty.

All the defendants were convicted, but Elizabeth Proctor was spared execution. She was pregnant, and it was thought wrong to kill an innocent life still in the womb. (Such ethical concerns disappeared once a child was born. Two babies died in prison during the trials.) On August 19, the rest of the prisoners were taken on the now well-trodden route to Gallows Hill. The huge crowd included Cotton Mather on horseback. He must have felt his presence might be needed to counteract the effects on the crowd of the prisoners' last words.

Those who confessed and were spared

It became apparent fairly early in the witch hunt that the way to save one's life, if one was accused, was by making a confession. But this was not clear from the start. In previous cases of witchcraft in New England, confessors had been sentenced to hang despite their confessions. Remarkably, even later confessors were mainly responding to other pressures than the sheer fear of death. The vast majority of the accused did not confess even though this meant they might die. It seems that those who did confess had been leaned on particularly hard by the magistrates and ministers. In the first four months of the witch hunt, these authorities handpicked people they thought most likely to succumb and threatened them with irons, the dungeon, and hanging. The five confessors from March to early July were two slaves, two adolescent girls, and the simple-minded mother of one of those girls. Later in the witch hunt, from July to September, when Cotton Mather and the judges badly needed more confessors to give the prosecution credibility for the trials, fifty more confessed. Almost all were from Andover. Thomas Barnard, the young minister, was active in getting people arrested. If he could not persuade prisoners with words, they were tortured, either by being bound "neck and heels" or being kept awake and upright for long periods. Confessions were drawn up for them, which they signed. Many later recanted.

Farewells

HE WAS RIGHT. All the men and women made moving, disquieting speeches. They "protested their innocency as in the presence of the great God, whom forthwith they were to appear before: they wished, and declared their wish, that their blood might be the last innocent blood shed upon that account. With great affection [emotion] they entreated Mr. Cotton Mather to pray with them: they prayed that God would discover what witchcraft were among us; they forgave

---

The first and most important confessor was Tituba, Samuel Parris's Native American slave. By confessing, she enabled the witch hunt to escalate from a small-scale affair to a dimension previously unknown in New England. The records make it abundantly clear that at her examination she was pressured into saying what the magistrates wanted to hear. Even before the examination, Samuel Parris had beaten her and "otherways abuse[d] her" to make her confess.[46]

Among the other early confessors were Abigail and Deliverance Hobbs, a mother and daughter subjected to especially strong pressure because they were vulnerable characters (Abigail was wild and attention-seeking and Deliverance fearful) and because they had been in Maine with the Reverend George Burroughs and could testify against him. Abigail Hobbs was tried and condemned on September 17 but reprieved. Deliverance was never tried. Both were released in April 1693.

The other early confessors were brave Margaret Jacobs, who later recanted, and the black slave Candy, whose mistress was also accused but did not confess. Candy was found not guilty by the Superior Court in January 1693.

The first five confessors from Andover were Ann Foster, seventy-two; her daughter Mary (Foster) Lacey, forty; her granddaughter Mary Lacey, eighteen; and Richard and Andrew Carrier, eighteen and fifteen, Martha Carrier's sons. There would be forty-five more.

---

their accusers; they spake without reflection on jury and judges, for bringing them in guilty, and condemning them; they prayed earnestly for pardon for all other sins, and for an interest in the precious blood of our dear Redeeemer; and seemed to be very sincere, upright, and sensible of their circumstances on all accounts; especially Proctor and Willard, whose whole management of themselves, from the gaol to the gallows, and whilst at the gallows, was very affecting and melting to the hearts of some considerable spectators."[47]

John Proctor pleaded for more time, saying he was not fit to die, but died nobly all the same. Most impressive of all was Reverend George Burroughs. He made an eloquent speech, declaring his innocence. His prayers were well worded, calm yet fervent, drawing tears from the crowd. He finished by reciting the Lord's Prayer without fault. Since the perfect or imperfect recitation of this prayer was viewed in the Court of Oyer and Terminer as a test of innocence or guilt, Burroughs's repeating it perfectly was disquieting. The accusing girls shouted that the devil was dictating it to him. As soon as Burroughs was dead, Cotton Mather addressed the crowd, while mounted on his horse, saying Burroughs was "no ordained minister" but was guilty as charged and that the devil "has often been transformed into an angel of light."[48] Only because Cotton Mather exerted all his personal power and authority over the crowd could the executions go on.

Like the rest of those hanged, Rev. Burroughs was buried in a crevice in the rocks, "his shirt and breeches . . . pulled off and an old pair of trousers, of one executed, put on his lower parts." He was interred in the same place as Willard and Carrier, with "one of his hands and his chin, and a foot of one [of] them being left uncovered."[49]

September 1692
Desperate measures

Andover touch test

THE NEXT TRIALS were to take place on September 9. On September 7, the Reverend Thomas Barnard called to the Andover meetinghouse a large group of church members and subjected them to what is now known as the "Andover touch test." Six of them later signed a document that graphically described what occurred. They and twelve others, seven of them children, arrived in the meetinghouse to find the afflicted girls of Andover already in their seats. As they entered, the girls went into fits. The church members were blindfolded and made to touch the thrashing, shouting girls, who then appeared to get well again, supposedly because the witchcraft that afflicted them had flowed back to the witches. The eight women, three men, and seven children were immediately taken as prisoners to Salem. Their relations urged them to confess to witchcraft, in order to save themselves. Because of this as well as the harsh way the magistrates treated them, they said anything and everything they were asked to.

There were now fifty-five confessors in jail. The sheer number may have quelled doubts on the part of the jurymen considering their verdicts. On September 9, Martha Cory, Mary Easty, Alice Parker, Ann Pudeator, Dorcas Hoar, and Mary Bradbury were all found guilty of witchcraft. Dorcas Hoar and Mary Bradbury were spared hanging, Dorcas because she confessed, Mary Bradbury because she escaped; but the others would go to the gallows.

Mary Easty's petitions

BEST REMEMBERED of the group is Mary Easty, sister of Rebecca Nurse. All three sisters—Rebecca, Mary, and Sarah Cloyce, who had slammed the door to the meetinghouse during Rev. Parris's sermon—were pious, brave, and intelligent. At her examination on April 21, Mary had made her denials of witchcraft with such cogency and force that John Hathorne, uncharacteristically, had asked the girls if they were sure "this was the woman." After a stunned, frightened silence, Ann Putnam and Elizabeth Hubbard cried out, "Oh, Goody Easty, Goody Easty, you are the woman, you are the woman."[50]

In May, for no apparent reason Mary Easty was "cleared by the afflicted persons" and let out of jail.[51] On her release, the girls had unusually spectacular fits. Mercy Lewis claimed that Mary Easty had almost killed her. "Dear Lord receive my soul," she cried out, "Let them not kill me quite."[52] Three days later, Mary Easty was taken back in again. Probably two factors caused her release and rejailing: the growing opposition to the witch hunt and Governor Phips's arrival. The Putnams may have wanted to demonstrate, to the population in general and the new governor in particular, the mayhem a released witch could cause. They probably picked on Mary Easty because she was so well respected. On the other hand, she was not quite as well connected and revered as her sister Rebecca. Rejailing Rebecca might have aroused opposition too powerful.

In August or September, with her trial in prospect, Mary Easty, with Sarah Cloyce, sent a petition to the court asking the judges to please act as their counsel, since they were allowed neither to plead their own cause nor use counsel to speak for them. They also asked that the pastor and church members of Topsfield, who knew them better than anyone, be allowed to speak in their favor. Finally, they pleaded that

Petition to the court by Mary Easty and Sarah Cloyce. (Courtesy, Peabody Essex Museum)

they should not be condemned by "the testimony of . . . such as are afflicted . . . without other legal evidence." They asked the honored court and jury not to condemn them "without a fair and equal hearing of what may be said for us, as well as against us."[53]

Their plea was in vain. As it happened, for reasons unknown to us, Sarah Cloyce was not brought to trial, but Mary Easty was condemned. Before her execution, she wrote another petition, one of the most moving historical documents to survive from the witch hunt. It began, "I petition to your honours not for my own life for I know I must die and my appointed time is set . . ." and went on to urge that the judges examine the "afflicted persons" and "confessing witches," as she was sure they were lying. She ended, "The Lord above who is the searcher of all hearts knows that as I shall answer it at the tribunal seat that I know not the least thing of witchcraft, therefore I cannot, I dare not, bely my own soul. I beg your honours not to deny this my humble petition from a poor dying innocent person and I question not but the Lord will give a blessing to your endeavours."[54]

More weight

ON SEPTEMBER 19, Giles Cory, husband of Martha, was pressed to death, by means of rocks loaded on his chest. This barbaric mode of execution was his punishment for refusing to enter a plea. It was the old English procedure called "peine forte et dure," which was meant to force from the prisoner the word "guilty" or "innocent." Giles's reasons for standing mute at the bar are not known. The suggestion that he was trying to prevent the seizure of his land cannot be right since he had already given everything he owned to his sons. He simply may have decided to refuse to cooperate with a court that had tricked him into helping condemn his own wife.

It took Giles hours to die. His ribs had to crack before the breath could be squeezed from his lungs. Towards the end, his tongue protruded from his mouth, and the sheriff pushed it back in again with the end of his cane. Tradition has it that the only words Giles Cory uttered during his torture were, "More weight, more weight."

Firebrands of hell

THE LAST HANGINGS took place three days later. Of the fifteen recently condemned, eight were executed. The other seven were reprieved, one because of pregnancy, the others as confessors. The convicted who died on September 22 were

Mary Easty, Alice Parker, Martha Cory, Ann Pudeator, Margaret Scott of Rowley, Wilmott Redd of Marblehead, and Samuel Wardwell and Mary Parker of Andover. Wardwell and Parker were the only Andover prisoners, apart from Martha Carrier, who refused to confess. On September 22, the cart set off from Salem prison with its heaviest load yet. It is scarcely surprising that as it was going up the hill it got stuck. The afflicted girls and others shouted that "the devil hindered it."[55]

It seems that the accusers were as afraid as ever that the condemned might win sympathy. They seized every opportunity to insult and mock the accused. As Wardwell spoke on the ladder, protesting his innocence, tobacco smoke from the executioner's pipe wafted into his face and made him splutter and cough. The afflicted girls shouted that the devil was stopping him from speaking. When the executioner's task was completed, the fanatical Nicholas Noyes turned towards the bodies suspended from the tree and said, "What a sad thing it is to see eight firebrands of hell hanging there."[56]

This may have misfired, winning sympathy rather than contempt. Martha Cory, protesting her innocence, had ended her life with an "eminent prayer."[57] Mary Easty's farewell to her husband, children, and friends was "as serious, religious, distinct and affectionate as could well be expressed, drawing tears from the eyes of almost all present."[58] Neither she nor any of the rest may have seemed to the crowd much of a "firebrand of hell." These were the last hangings. Perhaps partly because of their adverse effect on the crowd, the tide turned against the witch hunt.

Growing doubts

ENTHUSIASM FOR THE HUNT had been ebbing over the summer, as the voices of skepticism grew clearer and louder. In August, a respected resident of Salisbury, Massachusetts,

Brave words of some of the accused who were executed,
as displayed on the memorial in Danvers

"I am an innocent person. I never had to do with witchcraft since I was born. I am a gospel woman."—Martha Cory, March 21, 1692, at her examination

"The Lord above knows my innocency . . . as at the great day (it) will be known to men and angels."—Mary Easty, September 1692, in prison awaiting execution

"If it was the last moment I was to live, God knows I am innocent." —Elizabeth Howe, May 31, 1692, at her examination

"Well! Burn me or hang me, I will stand in the truth of Christ." —George Jacobs, May 10, 1692, at his examination

"Amen, Amen. A false tongue will never make a guilty person." —Susannah Martin, May 2, 1692, at her examination

"I can say before my eternal father I am innocent, and God will clear my innocency." —Rebecca Nurse, March 24, 1692, at her examination

"The magistrates, ministers, juries, and all the people in general, being so much enraged and incensed against us by the delusion of the devil, which we can term no other, by reason we know in our own consciences, we are all innocent persons."—John Proctor, July 23, 1692, in prison awaiting trial

"I fear not but the Lord in his due time will make me as white as snow."—John Willard, May 18, 1692, at his examination

Maj. Robert Pike, wrote a vigorous letter to magistrate Jonathan Corwin questioning the use of spectral evidence. He gave incisive voice to the view that Satan was capable of disguising himself as an innocent person in order to afflict and tempt others. Meanwhile, one of Boston's most eminent ministers, Samuel Willard, was criticizing the trials and even may have helped prisoners escape. At the end of September, he published, under a pseudonym, a pamphlet titled, *Some Miscellany Observations Respecting Witchcraft in a Dialogue between S and B*. Written in question-and-answer form, the pamphlet posed queries about the evidence needed to make convictions of witchcraft. To the answer that less evidence was required to prove witchcraft than murder because "how else shall witches be detected and punished according to God's command . . . ," he responded, "That is a dangerous principle, and contrary to the mind of God."

The only proof of witchcraft that Willard admitted as sufficient was a full confession by someone in his right mind who has not been frightened or coerced. Willard pointedly observed that there were many other means of coercion than those of the Spanish Inquisition.

October 1692–May 1693
Turning of the tide

Cases of conscience

IN OCTOBER came the most important of the works that helped stop the witch hunt. This was Increase Mather's *Cases of Conscience concerning Evil Spirits Personating Men*. At the request of the Association of Ministers in Boston, increasingly alarmed by the misery and chaos caused by the trials and hangings, he again addressed the question of evidence. Arriving at the same conclusion as the earlier *Return of Several Ministers Consulted*, that spectral evidence cannot be relied on, he expressed it now without ambiguity, saying nothing about the need for the speedy, vigorous prosecution of witches. Instead he stated, "It were better that ten suspected witches should escape, than that one innocent person should be condemned."[59]

This work was presented to the ministers on October 3.

The trials had been suspended, but they were due to start again in November.

Thomas Brattle's letter

ON OCTOBER 8, another excellent prose work, sharply critical of spectral evidence and the tests of witchcraft used at Salem, began circulating among people with power and influence. This was Thomas Brattle's "Letter." The author was a merchant and an eminent scientist, a member of the Royal Society, and the treasurer of Harvard College. The letter performs an elegant hatchet job on the attitudes, methods, and good faith of the Court of Oyer and Terminer.

Brattle intended his letter to get the attention of the General Court, scheduled to meet on October 12 to discuss the Salem trials. Though addressed to an unknown recipient, the letter was meant to reach the eyes of Governor Phips and his council. It undoubtedly did so, together with Mather's *Cases of Conscience*. On October 12, Phips forbade further

❖ ────────────────────────────────

Thomas Brattle's Letter

In a wonderful letter over fourteen pages long, Thomas Brattle criticized all aspects of the trials. Here are two excerpts. On the inability to shed tears as a sign of guilt of witchcraft, he argued persuasively:

"Some of the Salem gentlemen are very forward to censure and condemn the poor prisoner at the bar, because he sheds no tears: but such betray great ignorance in the nature of passion, and as great heedlessness as to common passages of a man's life. Some there are who never shed tears; others there are that ordinarily shed tears upon light occasions, and yet for their lives cannot shed a tear when the deepest sorrow is upon their hearts; and who is there that knows not these things? Who knows not that an ecstasy of joy will sometimes fetch tears, when as the quite contrary passion will shut them close up? Why then should

❖ ────────────────────────────────

Tomb of Thomas Brattle, whose letter of October 8, 1692, helped end the witch hysteria. King's Chapel Burying Ground. (Ralph Turcotte photo)

imprisonments for witchcraft, and on October 29 he dissolved the Court of Oyer and Terminer.

any be so silly and foolish as to take an argument from this appearance?"[60]

On the alleged ability of the accusers to see specters with their eyes shut:

"These afflicted persons do say, and often have declared it, that they can see specters when their eyes are shut, as well as when they are open.... I am sure they lie, at least speak falsely, if they say so; for the thing, in nature, is an utter impossibility. It is true, they may strongly fancy, or have things represented to their imaginations, when their eyes are shut; and I think this is all which ought to be allowed these blind, nonsensical girls.... The witches' meeting, the devil's baptism, and mock sacraments, which they oft speak of, are nothing else but the effect of their fancy, depraved and deluded by the devil, and not a reality to be regarded or minded by any wise man."[61]

Wonders

THE FORCES OF BIGOTRY and superstition had been dealt a death blow. But it would be a while yet before they expired. As Increase Mather was writing his *Cases of Conscience*, his son Cotton was finishing a long, diffuse work called *Wonders of the Invisible World*, commissioned in mid-June by Governor Phips, probably at the suggestion of William Stoughton. The core of the book is an account of five of the witch trials taken from records provided by Stephen Sewall, clerk of the court. The trials chosen—those of Bridget Bishop, Susannah Martin, Elizabeth Howe, Martha Carrier, and George Burroughs—included more nonspectral evidence than most. The authorities were anxious to show the accused had been rightly convicted. Sewall and Stoughton added a note saying, "We find the matters of fact and evidence truly reported."[62]

Although the "reporting" may have been accurate, the author's bias is clear. After his description of Bridget Bishop's being taken into the courtroom and the girls going into fits, Cotton Mather wrote, "There was little occasion to prove the witchcraft, it being evident and notorious to all beholders."[63] He saw fit to observe that "this rampant hag, Martha Carrier, was the person of whom the confessions of the witches and of her own children among the rest agreed that the devil had promised her she should be Queen of Hell."[64]

Wonders of the Invisible World was presented to William Phips at roughly the same time as Brattle's letter and Increase Mather's *Cases of Conscience*. But with nineteen people hanged, one pressed to death, one hundred fifty in jail, and another two hundred still at large but accused, Governor Phips badly wanted the madness to end. Ironically, the accusing girls had sharpened his desire. They had begun naming people as powerful as the two sons of former governor Simon Bradstreet, the wife of the Reverend John Hale of Beverly, and the wife of Governor Phips himself. Cotton Mather's

Wonders could not compete with the forces bringing the witch hunt to an end.

The turning of the tide did not bring sudden enlightenment. No one in authority seemed fully to grasp that all those hanged had been innocent. There was general confusion and defensiveness. All too often the colony's leaders seemed to care more about the repercussions for themselves personally than about justice. Governor Phips wrote letters to the government in England justifying his actions and blaming William Stoughton for the chaos. John Hale was soon penning his defense, *A Modest Enquiry into the Nature of Witchcraft*, published after he died. Cotton Mather displayed hysterical defensiveness in a new volume, *More Wonders of the Invisible World*. This became the title of Robert Calef's corruscating account of the witch trials, which included Mather's book, published in 1700.

The turned tide flowed slowly. It took until November for the afflicted girls to cease making accusations. Their death knell as witch finders came when they were called to Gloucester to investigate a suspected bewitching and, crossing Ipswich Bridge, met an old woman and went into fits. Instead of turning on the accused, the passers-by simply hurried on. The girls' power was gone.

New witch court

BUT THE TRIALS were not over. On December 6, an act was passed to allow a special session of the newly created Superior Court to try the remaining accused witches. Governor Phips appointed William Stoughton chief judge. However much Phips had criticised Stoughton's actions and advice, he still relied on him. The first session of the court on January 3 included four of the same judges as the Court of Oyer and Terminer. But there was a crucial difference now: spectral evidence was no longer admissable. Without the

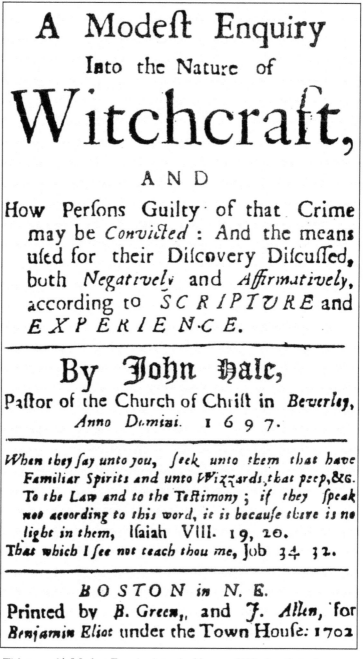

A Modeſt Enquiry

Into the Nature of

Witchcraft,

A N D

How Perſons Guilty of that Crime may be *Convicted* : And the means uſed for their Diſcovery Diſcuſſed, both *Negatively* and *Affirmatively*, according to *SCRIPTURE* and *EXPERIENCE*.

By John Hale,

Paſtor of the Church of Chriſt in *Beverley*, *Anno Domini.* 1 6 9 7.

When they ſay unto you, ſeek unto them that have Familiar Spirits and unto Wizzards, that peep, &c. To the Law and to the Teſtimony ; if they ſpeak not according to this word, it is becauſe there is no light in them, Iſaiah VIII. 19, 20.
That which I ſee not teach thou me, Job 34. 32.

B O S T O N in N. E.
Printed by *B. Green,* and *J. Allen,* for *Benjamin Eliot* under the Town Houſe: 1702

Title page of A Modest Enquiry into the Nature of Witchcraft *by the Reverend John Hale of Beverly. (Courtesy of the Beverly Historical Society and Museum, Beverly, Mass.)*

presence of the afflicted girls having fits, the jury could not believe that the ordinary-looking people before them were servants of the devil. Of the twenty-six tried, only three were found guilty. Two of these, Francis Dane's granddaughter Elizabeth Johnson and Mary Post of Rowley, were "the most senseless and ignorant creatures that could be found."[65] Perhaps in their senselessness and ignorance they repeated rambling confessions. The third woman found guilty, Sarah Wardwell, may also have repeated a former confession, since her husband Samuel had been hanged after going back on his. She may not have known that the former policy was reversed, and those making confessions were now sentenced to die.

Ultimately, Governor Phips granted reprieves for these three and for five other accused witches sentenced earlier by the Court of Oyer and Terminer. When word of this was brought to the Superior Court, William Stoughton was "enraged and filled with passionate anger" and walked off the bench. He shouted, "We were in a way to have cleared the land. . . . Who it is that obstructs the course of justice I know not; the Lord be merciful to the country."[66]

No more convictions

AFTER JANUARY 1693, no more accused witches were found guilty. In May, Governor Phips ordered that all those still in jail be released. About 150 people emerged to breathe fresh air for the first time in months. However, many remained locked away because they could not pay their prison fees. Brave young Margaret Jacobs was one of those detained, but in due course a stranger paid her bill out of pity. Later, he sued her for the sum, and she repaid him. Among those released in May was the woman who had been in prison longer than anyone, Samuel Parris's slave Tituba. The minister paid her jail fees with money from the new owner he sold her to. We do not know who the new owner was or where

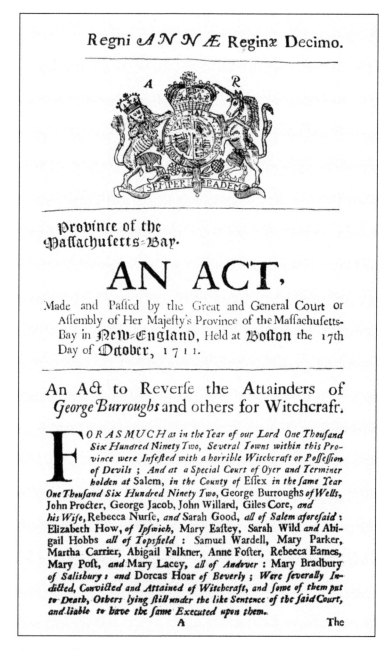

Regni *ANNÆ* Reginæ Decimo.

A   R

Province of the Massachusetts-Bay.

AN ACT,

Made and Passed by the Great and General Court or
Assembly of Her Majesty's Province of the Massachusetts-
Bay in New-England, Held at Boston the 17th
Day of October, 1711.

An Act to Reverse the Attainders of *George Burroughs* and others for Witchcraft.

FOR AS MUCH *as in the Year of our Lord One Thousand
Six Hundred Ninety Two, Several Towns within this Province were Infested with a horrible Witchcraft or Possession
of Devils ; And at a Special Court of Oyer and Terminer
holden at* Salem, *in the County of* Essex *in the same Year
One Thousand Six Hundred Ninety Two,* George Burroughs *of Wells,*
John Procter, George Jacob, John Willard, Giles Core, *and
his Wife,* Rebecca Nurse, *and* Sarah Good, *all of* Salem *aforesaid* :
Elizabeth How, *of* Ipswich, Mary Eastey, Sarah Wild *and* Abigail Hobbs *all of* Topsfield : Samuel Wardell, Mary Parker,
Martha Carrier, Abigail Falkner, Anne Foster, Rebecca Eames,
Mary Post, *and* Mary Lacey, *all of* Andover : Mary Bradbury
of Salisbury : *and* Dorcas Hoar *of* Beverly ; *Were severally In-
dicted, Convicted and Attained of Witchcraft, and some of them put
to Death, Others lying still under the like Sentence of the said Court,
and liable to have the same Executed upon them.*

A   The

First page of An Act to Reverse the Attainders of George Burroughs and others
for Witchcraft, *passed by the General Court at Boston on October 17, 1711.
(Courtesy, Danvers Archival Center, Danvers, Mass.)*

Tituba went. Of those jailed with her, Sarah Good had been hanged and Sarah Osborne had perished in prison.

Guilt of innocent blood

THE AFTERMATH of the witch hunt was painful and prolonged. The Reverend Samuel Parris stayed in Salem Village for another five years. In November 1694, he read a statement in the meetinghouse titled "Meditations for Peace," admitting that he had given too much weight to spectral evidence and may have spoken unadvisedly. But it was far too little, too late, for the relations of Rebecca Nurse and the others he had helped cause to die. In September 1697, after an arbitration by three Boston ministers on the issues of his back pay and the deeds to the parsonage, he was at last forced to leave Salem Village.

The last part of his life was no more successful than the first, except that after his wife Elizabeth died, Parris remarried. His new wife was a woman of means, easing the effects of his failures. His daughter Betty eventually married, as did several other of the afflicted girls. Abigail Williams disappeared from the records after July 1692 and may well have died, perhaps by her own hand, not long after. She was almost certainly the accuser John Hale refers to as being "followed by diabolical manifestations to her death."[67]

Grudging amends

FOR THOSE HUNDREDS of people whose lives, one way or another, had been ruined by the witch hunt, restitution came late, if at all. The first pleas were purely for reinstatement of character. In 1700, Abigail Falkner of Andover, condemned and then reprieved, asked the General Court for "defacing of the record" on the grounds that the only testimony against her was that of spectral evidence, which had since been discredited.[68] Her plea was not granted. A similar petition was

presented in 1702 by a long list of people who had been convicted, together with relations of people who had been
hanged, including Mary Easty's husband and one of John
Proctor's sons. The Massachusetts House of Representatives
passed a bill forbidding the use of spectral evidence in the
future and declaring that "the infamy and reproach cast on
the names and posterity" of those found guilty because of it
should "in some measure be rolled away."[69] This grudging
resolution scarcely met the petitioners' needs. A year and four
months later, a group of Essex County ministers sent an
address to the General Court describing the afflicted girls as
"young persons under diabolical molestations"[70] and asking it
to grant the petitioners' request to clear their names. Among
the signatories was Joseph Green, who in 1697 had replaced
Samuel Parris as pastor of Salem Village. Nicholas Noyes did
not sign. The General Court still did nothing.

Six years later, on May 25, 1709, another petition was presented by some of the same people, together with others.
This plea asked for financial remuneration as well as the
restoration of the victims' good names. A new signatory was
Phillip English, who gave a detailed account of articles that
had been seized from his warehouses, wharf, and shop. He
also listed the expenses incurred by him and his wife during
their nine weeks in prison and in escaping from prison. Even
now, nothing was done.

In September of the following year, Mary Easty's husband
presented a memorandum to the General Court asking for
remuneration for the loss of his "beloved wife," though, he
said, "My sorrow and trouble of heart in being deprived of
her in such a manner" could never truly be compensated.[71]
Relations of Elizabeth Howe, Sarah Wildes, Mary Bradbury,
Edward and Sarah Bishop, George Burroughs, Giles and
Martha Cory, and Rebecca Nurse all sent petitions. At last, in
October 1711, the General Court passed an act reversing the

convictions of those for whom family members had pleaded. It did not extend the reversal to those who had been hanged for witchcraft but for whom no petitions were made. These included Bridget Bishop, Susannah Martin, Alice Parker, Ann Pudeator, Wilmott Redd, and Margaret Scott.

On December 17, 1711, the sum of £578/12 was granted to the petitioning relatives. By far the largest amount, £150, went to the Proctors, since John Proctor had been the most prosperous of those hanged. The second largest, £79, went to the heirs of George Jacobs Senior, and the third, £50, to those of George Burroughs. But the size of the rest of the amounts shows no clear rationale. The relatives of the fairly prosperous Elizabeth Howe got only £12, while William Good, husband of the destitute Sarah, got £30. Wild Abigail Hobbs was given £10, despite being an accuser as well as one of the accused. Altogether, the relations of twenty-four people who were executed, died in prison, or spent a long time there were compensated.

Meanwhile, other wrongs were righted. In 1703, Joseph Green, Salem Village's new minister, reversed Martha Cory's excommunication. In 1712 Salem church negated the excommunications of Rebecca Nurse and Giles Cory.

But justice had still not been done. There were many others who had suffered just as badly and as yet received nothing. At the end of 1738 a son of Samuel Sewall, also named Samuel, chaired a committee formed to obtain information relating to "the circumstances of the persons and families who suffered in the calamity of the times in and about the year 1692."[72] The records leave unclear what the result of this action was. But not long afterward, the sum of £200 was allowed to the heirs of Phillip English. It is ironic that English never knew that a part of the remuneration he had been vigorously demanding for years was finally granted. He had sued George Corwin for the illegal seizure of his property to the value of £1,500, but lost the case. He brought another suit that was outstanding when Corwin died in 1697. English's rage against the sheriff was such that he said he would seize Corwin's body to satisfy the debt. The corpse had to be interred on the Corwin property, where English could not reach it.

It took until 1957 for the Massachusetts State Legislature to approve a resolution exonerating the six accused witches not included in the reversal of 1711. But of the six, the only one named was Ann Pudeator. Bridget Bishop, Alice Parker, Margaret Scott, Wilmott Redd, and Susannah Martin at last achieved justice on October 31, 2001, when a bill exonerating them by name was signed by acting Massachusetts governor Jane Swift.

Apologies at last

RESTITUTIONS TOOK SO LONG in part because at no point was there clear, universal recognition that a huge wrong had been done. Admittedly, certain people felt a burden of guilt and said they were sorry. The twelve men who had sat on several of the juries in the summer of 1692, including the one that changed the verdict on Rebecca Nurse, wrote a paper asking forgiveness for "ignorantly and unwittingly" bringing upon themselves and their people "the guilt of innocent blood."[73] The minister Samuel Sewall delivered a paper to the General Court saying that he desired to take the blame for setting up the Court of Oyer and Terminer. He did this at an assembly called on a day of fasting, January 14, 1697, to atone for all New England's sins. But the proclamation announcing the fast avoided the issue, referring to "whatever mistakes on either hand have been fallen into, either by the body of this people, or any orders of men, referring to the late tragedy raised among us by Satan and his instruments."[74] The official government line on the witch hunt was that innocent people may have died and guilty ones escaped; the whole thing was deeply regrettable; and no one was to blame.

Certainly no one was ever held to account. John Hathorne and William Stoughton continued their careers as politicians and merchants; both lived to old age. Cotton Mather became ever more paranoid but continued as a minister until he died in his sixties. Thomas Putnam and his wife farmed in Salem Village until they both died in early middle age.

One apology was made, though, that may have eased the hurt of some of those who had suffered most deeply. In 1706, Ann Putnam, now twenty-six and having survived both of her parents, stood in the Salem Village meetinghouse in front of a packed congregation, including the Nurse children and grandchildren, and listened to the popular new minister, Joseph Green, read out a statement. He may have helped her write it, but he read it as hers:

> I desire to be humbled before God for that sad and humbling providence that befell my father's family in the year about '92; that I, then being in my childhood, should, by such a providence of God, be made an instrument for the accusing of several persons of a grievous crime, whereby their lives were taken away from them whom now I have just grounds and good reason to believe they were innocent persons; and that it was a great delusion of Satan that deceived me in that sad time, whereby I justly fear I have been instrumental, with others, though ignorantly and unwittingly, to bring upon myself and this land the guilt of innocent blood; though what was said or done by me against any person I can truly and uprightly say, before God and man, I did it not out of any anger, malice, or ill-will to any person, for I had no such thing against one of them; but what I did was ignorantly, being deluded by Satan. And partic- ularly, as I was a chief instrument of accusing of

Goodwife Nurse and her two sisters, I desire to lie in the dust, and to be humbled for it, in that I was a cause, with others, of so sad a calamity to them and their families; for which I desire to lie in the dust, and earnestly beg forgiveness of God, and from all those unto whom I have given just cause of sorrow and offence, whose relations were taken away or accused.[75]

Ann died, unmarried, eleven years later.

The descendants of Thomas Putnam disappeared from Salem Village. In 1752, Salem Village became Danvers, an entity separate from Salem Town, as the Putnams had desired. By that time, the values the Town stood for—enterprise, freedom, and tolerance—had imbued the whole of society. Ironically, the Salem witch trials, which constituted an attempt to keep old-fashioned Puritanism alive, helped to kill it.

The jurors' apology

The twelve men who had sat on several of the 1692 juries, including the one that reversed Rebecca Nurse's verdict, showed they had acted in good faith when they later signed a statement expressing their sorrow at their fatal mistakes:

"We confess that we ourselves were not capable to understand, nor able to withstand the mysterious delusions of the powers of darkness, and prince of the air; but were for want of knowledge in ourselves, and better information from others, prevailed with to take up with such evidence against the accused, as on further consideration, and better information, we justly fear was insufficient for the touching the lives of any . . . whereby we fear we have been instrumental with others, though ignorantly and unwittingly, to bring upon ourselves, and this people of the Lord, the guilt of innocent blood . . .

The Twenty Innocents
Who Were Executed

OF THE ACCUSED who refused to confess, nineteen were hanged and one was pressed to death. It is a remarkable fact that for the most part it took intense psychological pressure and physical torture to extract confessions from prisoners. At last, after three centuries, the twenty people who died are honored by two splendid memorials, one in Salem, one in Danvers. Some of their names are well known, some less so. All deserve the profoundest respect for their honesty and courage.

❖ *Bridget Bishop*, fifty-two, the wife of a Salem lawyer, Edward Bishop, was the first accused witch to be hanged, on June 10. She had a long-standing reputation for witchcraft. She has been confused with the Sarah (Wildes) Bishop of Beverly who kept a tavern and was accused of

---

"And do hereby declare that we justly fear that we were sadly deluded and mistaken, for which we are much disquieted and distressed in our minds; and do therefore humbly beg forgiveness, first of God for Christ's sake for this our error; and pray that God would not impute the guilt of it to ourselves, nor others; and we also pray that we may be considered candidly, and aright by the living sufferers as being then under the power of a strong and general delusion, utterly unacquainted with, and not experienced in matters of that nature.

"We do heartily ask forgiveness of you all, whom we have justly offended, and do declare according to our present minds, we would none of us do such things again on such grounds for the whole world; praying you to accept of this in way of satisfaction for our offence; and that you would bless the inheritance of the Lord, that he may be entreated for the land."[76]

---

witchcraft by John Hale. Sarah Bishop and her husband, also named Edward, were examined and imprisoned but escaped.

✧ *George Burroughs*, forty-two, was, of all those hanged, the one the magistrates and ministers most wished to see die. He was a dissident pastor who preached to Anglicans and Baptists as well as Puritans and who had not even had his own children baptized. The persecutors went to great lengths to produce evidence against him, in the form of confessions stating that he had presided at witch meetings and was trying to establish Satan's kingdom in New England.

Born into a well-to-do family in Suffolk, England, in 1650, Burroughs had been brought to Virginia as a baby and a few years later taken to Massachusetts, to be raised by his mother in Roxbury. Having graduated from Harvard College in 1670, he preached in Falmouth, Maine, until an Indian attack in August 1676 forced him to flee. After a period as minister in Salisbury, Massachusetts, he came as pastor to Salem Village, where he buried his first wife and married his second, the widow of John Hathorne's brother. His second wife died in 1691, and he married again a year later. Burroughs remained in Salem Village for less than three years, leaving after deep disagreements with Thomas Putnam and his allies. He returned to Maine but in May 1692 was brought back to Salem Village under arrest. He was convicted on August 5 and hanged, with four others, on August 19. He made an eloquent speech protesting his innocence and recited the Lord's Prayer without fault. This so moved the onlookers that, when he was dead, Cotton Mather had to use all his authority to continue the executions. He claimed that Burroughs was not a properly ordained minister and that the devil could disguise himself as "an angel of light."[77]

✧ *Martha Carrier*, thirty-eight, was the first accused witch from Andover. Her brother-in-law, Roger Toothaker, of Billerica, Massachusetts, had been accused two weeks earlier.

At her examination she answered Hathorne with great courage and spirit, saying of the afflicted girls, "They will dissemble if I look upon them," and "It is a shameful thing that you should mind these folks that are out of their wits."[78] Her two sons Richard and Andrew were accused, imprisoned, and tortured before her trial, to make them confess and testify against her. Even her younger children, Thomas, ten, and Sarah, seven, were induced by Hathorne to say that their mother had made them witches. Martha was hanged on August 19 with George Burroughs and three others.

✤ *Martha Cory*, sixty-five, was the fourth person, and the first church member, to be accused as a witch. Respectably married and known to be pious, she nevertheless had a tainted reputation because she had once given birth to an illegitimate child. She was outspoken in her skepticism about the existence of witches in Salem Village. She was tried on September 9 and executed on September 22.

✤ *Giles Cory*, eighty, Martha Cory's husband, was a prosperous farmer with a reputation for aggression. In 1675, he was brought to court for helping cause the death of a manservant by beating him. In 1692, he testified against his third wife, Martha Cory, at her examination for witchcraft, saying that her presence had stopped him from praying. Soon afterwards he was arrested himself. When he was brought to trial, he chose to stand mute, refusing to plead guilty or innocent. As a result, on September 19 he was tortured to death by the old English method called "peine forte et dure." Rocks were loaded on his chest until his ribs cracked and he could no longer breathe.

✤ *Mary Easty*, fifty-eight, was one of three sisters who were accused and imprisoned. The others were Rebecca Nurse, hanged on July 19, and Sarah Cloyce, never brought to trial. They were the daughters of William Towne of

Memorials to Giles and Martha Cory on Lowell Street, Peabody, erected in 1992 on the three hundredth anniversary of the witch trials. (Ralph Turcotte photo)

Topsfield, who had been engaged in furious land disputes with the Putnams for years. Mary's husband, Isaac Easty, was also of Topsfield and an ally of her father. Mary was notable for writing two petitions from prison, one with her sister Sarah before she was tried, the other after she was condemned. The first was a well-argued, eloquent plea for a fair trial, the second an equally well argued and even more eloquent plea for the judges to reexamine their methods and beliefs. Mary said she did not "petition for my own life for I know I must die and my appointed time is set" but for the judges to examine the afflicted persons and confessors, instead of believing all they said, so that no more innocent people would die.[79] Mary was hanged on September 22.

✛ *Sarah Good*, thirty-nine, was one of the first three people accused, with Tituba and Sarah Osborne. Born in 1653 in Wenham, she was the daughter of a well-to-do innkeeper who committed suicide in 1672. He left a large estate to his widow, who then married a man who tried to disinherit her seven grown children. Sarah's lot worsened when she married an indentured servant who soon died, leaving huge debts.

After taking legal action, she was granted a share of her father's estate, but it was seized back to pay what her husband had owed. When she married again, it was to a laborer who rarely had work. She was a typical witch suspect in that she had gone down in the world, resented it, had to beg for necessities, and was bitter and ungrateful when given them. She had several children, one of whom, four-year-old Dorcas Good, was imprisoned for eight months. A babe in arms accompanied Sarah to prison and died there. Sarah was hanged on July 19. On the gallows, she said to the minister Nicholas Noyes, "I am no more a witch than you are a wizard, and if you take away my life, God will give you blood to drink."[80] Nicholas Noyes later died of a hemorrhage, bleeding from the mouth. Nathaniel Hawthorne used Sarah's curse in his novel, *The House of the Seven Gables*, attributing it to the fictional Thomas Maule. The character to whom it was spoken was Colonel Pyncheon, based on the magistrate John Hathorne (Nathaniel's great-great-grandfather). In the novel he dies a sudden, mysterious death, blood soaking his beard.

Elizabeth Howe, fifty-three, was the wife of James Howe, a nephew of the Reverend Francis Dane of Andover. They lived in Topsfield and were closely associated with the Towne family. At her trial ten witnesses testified to Elizabeth's practice of witchcraft in past years, but eleven people spoke in her favor. Her husband was blind, and Elizabeth's father-in-law said that she was "very careful, loving, obedient and kind, considering [my son's] want of eyesight, tenderly leading him about by the hand."[81] Elizabeth was hanged on July 19.

George Jacobs, eighty, was a prosperous landowner in Salem Village where he had lived for thirty-three years. He and his sixteen-year-old granddaughter Margaret were arrested together on May 10. His son, his son's wife, and her brother Daniel Andrew were accused four days later. One reason George Jacobs and his family were accused was almost certainly because Andrew was a close ally of the Porters and a prime Putnam enemy. At his examination, the crippled George Jacobs showed great courage and spirit, saying, "You tax me for a wizard, you may as well tax me for a buzzard, I have done no harm."[82] He was hanged on August 19.

✤ *Susannah Martin*, sixty-seven, a widow who lived in Amesbury, had a history of witchcraft accusations against her. At her examination she was contemptuous of the afflicted girls and their antics, laughing when Ann Putnam threw her glove at her. When asked why she laughed, she said, "Well I may at such folly." Showing close knowledge of the Bible, she said, "He that appeared in Samuel's shape, a glorified saint, may appear in anyone's shape."[83] She was referring to 1 Samuel 28, in which "the witch of Endor" raises the dead Samuel. Susannah was suggesting that "Samuel" was the devil in disguise, and if the devil could appear as him, he could appear as anyone. She was denying the reliability of spectral evidence with particular force. She was hanged on July 19.

✤ *Rebecca Nurse*, seventy-one, sister of Mary Easty and Sarah Cloyce, was targeted by the Putnams as a daughter of Joseph Towne, with whom they had fierce land disputes in Topsfield, and the wife of Francis Nurse, Towne's ally. Ann Putnam, as well as her daughter, claimed to be afflicted by Rebecca and went out of her way to see her arrested. Goodwife Nurse fitted the ideal of Puritan womanhood. She was hard-working, pious, and an exemplary mother and grandmother to eight children and their offspring. She and her husband had risen from humble beginnings, and by 1692 they possessed three hundred acres near the center of Salem Village. There was more resistance from the Salem Village community to her trial and conviction than to that of anyone else. A petition was mounted on her behalf, and signed by thirty-nine people. Eleven men and women deposed in her favor. The jury initially acquitted her but was induced to change its decision by the chief judge, William Stoughton. She was hanged on July 19.

✤ *Alice Parker* was the wife of a Salem mariner and fisherman. Mary Warren, who had just rejoined the accusers after spending three weeks in prison, provided most of the testimony against her. Mary claimed Alice had killed her sister and mother by witchcraft because Mary's father had promised to mow her grass but had not done so. She also claimed that Alice had caused the drowning of a number of mariners. The fanatical pastor Nicholas Noyes accused Alice of having as much as admitted she was a witch, but she steadfastly insisted on her innocence. She was hanged on September 22.

✤ *Mary Parker*, fifty-five, the widow of Nathan Parker of Andover, was one of the few Andover residents accused of witchcraft who refused to confess. Her twenty-two-year-old daughter was arrested in mid-August, and Mary was taken two weeks later. On September 7, her niece and great-niece were arrested after being subjected to the "Andover touch test." She was hanged on September 22. The attempt by George Corwin to seize her estate after her death met with failure, due to the clear thinking and courage of her two adult sons. They declared that she had left no estate, bribing Corwin to let the matter drop with a payment of £6.

✤ *Ann Pudeator*, sixty, had lived in Casco, Maine, with her first husband when George Burroughs was preacher there. Her husband had died in the 1676 Indian attack from which Burroughs narrowly escaped. Ann had remarried Jacob Pudeator, of Salem, who died in 1682. She was examined on July 2, and on July 26 her son, James Greenslade, was summoned from Casco to give evidence against George

Burroughs at his trial. There is no record of James's testimony, but on September 15 Ann's other son, Thomas, testified against Rev. Burroughs. His testimony seems to have been an attempt to save his mother's life, since Burroughs had been hanged a month earlier. Ann had been condemned on September 9, and on September 12 she had petitioned the court for a reconsideration of her case on the grounds that several of those who had testified against her were liars. She was hanged on September 22.

✢ *John Proctor*, sixty, is the most famous of the nineteen people hanged, due to Arthur Miller's play *The Crucible*. In the play, Proctor is shown having an affair with Abigail Williams. In real life, Proctor was sixty years old and Williams eleven. They probably never met except in court. Proctor was a prosperous farmer and tavernkeeper who was accused because of his outspoken contempt for the afflicted girls, shouting, "Hang them! Hang them!"[84] He wrote a letter from prison to the ministers in Boston, telling them of the physical torture Martha Carrier's sons and his own son William had undergone to elicit confessions. He was hanged on August 19.

✢ *Wilmott Redd*, born about 1638, was married to Samuel Redd, a Marblehead fisherman. At her trial, certain Marblehead citizens testified that she had committed witchcraft on a Mrs. Symmes, causing her to suffer constipation. Wilmott was hanged on September 22.

✢ *Margaret Scott*, seventy-one, the wife of Benjamin Scott of Rowley, was accused at her trial of hurting a Robert Shilleto by witchcraft for two or three years before he died, and afflicting a Frances Wycom earlier in the summer of 1692. She was hanged on September 22.

✤ *Samuel Wardwell*, forty-nine, of Andover, was arrested and imprisoned on August 15. On September 1, together with his wife, stepdaughter, and daughter, he made a confession. But on September 13 he retracted, saying he had lied and adding that it made no difference whether he confessed or not because he would die either way. By this stage of the witch hunt, confessors were being tried and condemned, though all were later reprieved. Wardwell was hanged on September 22.

✤ *Sarah (Averill) Wildes*, sixty-five, was the wife of John Wildes of Topsfield, who contended with the Putnams over land. Her son, Ephraim, the constable of Topsfield, claimed that Deliverance Hobbs had accused his mother of witchcraft because Hobbs was angry at his having arrested her. Numerous prior witchcraft accusations against Sarah were brought forward at her trial, including one from the Reverend John Hale, claiming she had bewitched someone he knew fifteen or sixteen years before. She was hanged on July 19.

✤ *John Willard*, thirty, a Salem Village farmer, fled to Lancaster, Massachusetts, to try to escape arrest but was followed and returned. At his trial, nine of his in-laws testified against him. He was hanged on August 19.

WHERE TO GO & WHAT TO SEE

Overview

START AT THE Salem Witch Museum. Located at the corner of Washington Square North and Boston Street, opposite Salem Common, the museum offers a twenty-minute show on the witch trials, with life-size figures and dramatic lighting and sound effects. The story is simplified but gives an excellent overview and a very good sense of the harshness and anxiety of life at the time and how much suffering the witch trials caused. The Witch Museum bookshop is the best in Salem for books and pamphlets on the trials.

The Old Burying Point on Charter Street, the oldest cemetery in Salem, is a five-minute walk from the Witch Museum. Several people connected to the trials are buried there, including John Hathorne, the magistrate. None of those executed are here, as they were buried where they were hanged, and their graves have never been found. However, a

Old Burying Point in Salem

Witchcraft Victims' Memorial in Danvers

Salem Witch Museum

The House of the Seven Gables in Salem

Memorial to Rebecca Nurse in Danvers

beautiful memorial to those twenty innocent victims was built next to the cemetery in 1992. Together, the cemetery and memorial form Salem's most evocative site.

From here, you may want to explore sites in the adjacent town of Danvers, formerly Salem Village. The most rewarding witch-trials site, the Rebecca Nurse Homestead, includes not only the house of the convicted Rebecca Nurse but also extensive grounds that are scarcely changed from three hundred years ago. It also comprises the Nurse family cemetery and a replica of the meetinghouse where the accused were examined. Nearby is the site of the parsonage where the hysteria began; Ingersoll's Ordinary, the Salem Village tavern where some of the pretrial examinations were held; and the moving Witchcraft Victims' Memorial.

If you can't get to Danvers but still have some time left in Salem, you could walk or drive to Gallows Hill. The site of the hangings isn't definitely known, but you can trace the route the condemned would have followed and look at two of the possible spots where the gallows or hanging tree may have stood.

For those who like to imagine places as they once were, from the layout of the streets and views in the distance, it is worth visiting the sites of the Salem Town courthouse and meetinghouse. The Salem Trolley gives an overview of Salem Town and in its commentary includes information about the

Bridget Bishop House in Danvers

North Andover Old Burying Ground

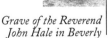

Wadsworth Burial Ground in Danvers

Grave of the Reverend John Hale in Beverly

Granary Burying Ground in Boston

trials. Also, the Jonathan Corwin house, now known as the Witch House, is the only building in Salem itself with a direct connection to the trials. It gives a good sense of the opulence of the class from which influential magistrates, such as Jonathan Corwin, were drawn.

For those who want to go farther afield than Salem and Danvers, North Andover's Old Burying Ground contains the stone-marked graves of many of those involved in the Andover witch hunt.

Salem

Salem Witch Museum

The Salem Witch Museum's Gothic appearance promises an intriguing exhibit, and what you find meets expectations. Visitors wait in a darkened auditorium until music starts and lights come up. Above, set in the wall, is a tableau of a farmhouse interior of 1692, with life-size figures sewing and spinning. The voice-over begins telling the story. The ensuing show, though simplified, is the best available introduction to the witch trials, bringing the events and people to life and

Salem Witch Museum.
(Ralph Turcotte photo)

giving an excellent overview of the conditions of the time, the course of events, and the resulting devastation.

The Salem Witch Museum also offers a display, called Witches: Evolving Perceptions, about witchcraft and witch hunts through the ages. Its other main attraction is an excellent bookstore. All the books and pamphlets suggested at the end of this guidebook can be bought there.

Salem Witch Museum, Washington Square North. 978-744-1692. www.salemwitchmuseum.com. Open daily year-round. Closed Thanksgiving, Christmas, New Year's Day. Admission fee.

Old Burying Point (Charter Street)

In 1692, the "burying point" started a hundred yards beyond the Charter Street entrance to the present-day cemetery, at the spot where now stands a bronze map locating the most interesting graves. The area between the entrance gate and the map, which now contains six marble-topped tombs, became part of the cemetery later. If you gaze ahead across the rough grass dotted with headstones toward Derby Street, you can easily imagine this place as it was in 1692. Beyond the low wall at the end, the ground sloped to the bank of the South River, which was wider then. This spot, which the first settlers chose as the most suitable in Salem for burying their dead, was a promontory. To the left, masts of ships would have risen where today we see signs with the words "Witch Village" and "The Witchcraft Hysteria of 1692." The wood frame house you see on your right was built in the early eighteenth century by the Peabody family. It was the home of Nathaniel Hawthorne's bride, Sophia Peabody.

Only a few of the grave markers visible today would have been standing in 1692 (because most were then built of wood, which has since decomposed). An unobtrusive headstone, about a hundred yards ahead beyond a prominent tomb, belongs to Mary Cory, Giles Cory's second wife.

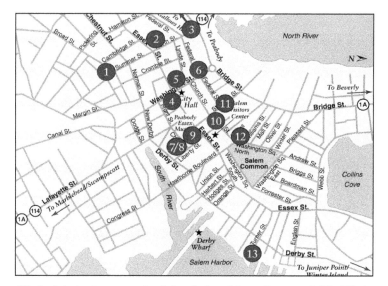

Witch trials sites in present-day Salem: **1.** *Broad Street Cemetery.* **2.** *The Witch House.* **3.** *Gallows Hill.* **4.** *Site of Salem Meetinghouse.* **5.** *Site of Salem Courthouse.* **6.** *Superior Court Building.* **7.** *Old Burying Point.* **8.** *Salem Witch Trials Memorial.* **9.** *Peabody Essex Museum.* **10.** *St. Peter's Church.* **11.** *Site of Old Salem Jail.* **12.** *Salem Witch Museum.* **13.** *The House of the Seven Gables.*

Giles's third wife, Martha, was hanged on September 22, 1692. He himself was pressed to death three days earlier. On the far left of the cemetery, about a third of the way toward Derby Street, is the grave containing the remains of Elinor Hollingsworth, the mother of Mary English, accused of witchcraft with her husband, Phillip English, the richest merchant in Salem. The couple were jailed but made their escape and were never brought to trial. To the right, with a diamond-shaped panel on its top, is the Gedney family tomb, in existence in 1692 though not yet the resting place of Bartholomew Gedney. One of the three magistrates of the witch trials, he was interred here in 1697. Near this tomb is the grave of John Turner, the sea captain and merchant who built the residence now known as The House of the Seven Gables. It was this dwelling that Hawthorne used as the model for the house in his novel.

John Hathorne himself is buried ahead of the bronze map, slightly to the left, under a headstone set in granite. It reads, "Here lyes inter'd ye body of Colo. John Hathorne Esq. Aged 76 years who died May 10th 1717." Hathorne was in large part responsible for the deaths of the nineteen people hanged and one pressed to death in 1692. He would have been horrified to know that three hundred years later, his remains would be lying within yards of a splendid memorial to the people he helped condemn.

To the right of the bronze map, past the nearest tomb, are the graves of two Samuel Shattucks, one of whom died in 1689, the other in 1695. One of them was the son, and one of them the father of the Samuel Shattuck who testified against Bridget Bishop, the first alleged witch to be hanged. He said she had given him some pieces of lace to dye which were so short that he could not imagine what she would use them for. The implication was that such lace must have clothed a witch's doll. He also testified that Bridget had cast a spell on one of his sons. The Samuel who died in 1695 was the child "bewitched" by Bridget Bishop.

Old Burying Point, Charter Street. Open dawn to dusk.

Salem Witch Trials Memorial

Adjoining the cemetery is the Salem Witch Trials Memorial, erected in 1992 for the tercentenary. It takes the unusual and imaginative form of twenty stone rectangles protruding horizontally inside a stone enclosure. Each is engraved with the name of one of those executed, and the means and date of his or her execution. A path runs beside the stones, enclosing a lawn and tall black locust trees (symbolizing execution). At the entrance, words spoken by those who were hanged are carved in granite set underfoot. The inscriptions are beginning to wear away now, but most are still legible, including

Stone bench dedicated to the memory of Giles Corey at the Salem Witch Trials Memorial. (Ralph Turcotte photo)

GILES COREY PRESSED TO DEATH SEPT. 19, 1692

the declaration, "God knows I am innocent. I am wholly innocent of such wickedness." Some are interrupted mid-sentence by the wall, suggesting lives cut short.

The memorial design, by Maggie Smith and James Cutler, was the winning entry in an international competition organized by the Salem Witch Trials Tercentenary Committee. Playwright Arthur Miller unveiled the design to the press and public in November 1991, and the memorial was dedicated on August 5, 1992, by Nobel laureate Elie Wiesel. It has won four national awards for excellence in construction and design.

Salem Witch Trials Memorial, Liberty Street, between Charter and Derby Streets.

Gallows Hill

No one knows for certain where nineteen people condemned as witches were hanged. But all the evidence contained in the surviving records, including death warrants, Samuel Sewall's diary, and Robert Calef's *More Wonders of the Invisible World*, points to the lower ledges of what is now called Gallows Hill. Charles W. Upham, author of the mid-nineteenth century tome *Salem Witchcraft*, was convinced that the executions took place at the summit. But he had to admit that nothing but tradition supported this. The evidence points further down the hill. In 1766, future U.S. president John Adams wrote in his diary while visiting Salem that someone had recently planted locust trees over the graves of the witches. We know that eighteen years before, Thorndike Proctor, grandson of the John Proctor who was hanged, had planted locust trees on the land between the present Proctor and Pope streets. One of Thorndike's descendants mentioned a cleft in the rocks that might have been the crevice where the hanged were interred. The locusts are all gone now, and the crevice is filled in. But what is now called Proctor's Ledge seems the best candidate for the hanging site.

Another possibility is that the executions took place even farther down the hill, where condominiums now stand. In 1783, part of a coffin was dug up by Benjamin Goodhue, who owned property there. But records indicate that the coffin was actually discovered nearer to where the locust trees stood. If that is so, the discovery supports the case for Proctor's Ledge.

PATH OF THE CONDEMNED

For visitors who prefer to drive, there is public parking at Gallows Hill Park. Those who wish to take an hour's walk can set out from the site of the old jail, at the crossing of St. Peter's Street and Federal Street, where the condemned were

Proctor's Ledge.
(Ralph Turcotte
photo)

brought from the dungeons and loaded into carts. In 1692,
St. Peter's Street, then called Prison Lane, ran all the way to
Essex Street. Today, Museum Place stands between the two,
so turn right along Church Street and take the first left down
to Essex Street. From that point you will follow the same
route as the condemned, along Essex Street to Boston Street,
and so to Gallows Hill. As you pass the intersection of Essex
Street and North Street, you'll see the only building still
standing that the condemned also would have seen: the residence of Jonathan Corwin, known today as the Witch
House. Corwin was one of the magistrates who examined
those accused of witchcraft and sent them to jail. Later he sat
as a judge on the Court of Oyer and Terminer and condemned some of them to death. We can only guess what they
felt, seeing his house.

Farther along Essex Street, where today stand nineteenth-
century houses, the condemned would have seen the orchards
and fields of large estates. Off Boston Street, now flanked by
commercial buildings, fields stretched to the right toward the
expanse of the North River. To the left, marshland covered

the few hundred feet to the same river, where it turned abruptly southward and narrowed. Beyond marsh and water was the towering hill where the gallows waited.

Turn left up Hanson Street and climb the steep hill to Gallows Hill Park, the execution site favored by historian Upham. It is also the site Nathaniel Hawthorne had in mind when he wrote his story "Alice Doane's Appeal," set in the early nineteenth century. He wrote,

> The eminence formed part of an extensive tract of pasture land, and was traversed by cow paths in various directions; but, strange to tell, though the whole slope and summit were of a peculiarly deep green, scarce a blade of glass was visible from the base upward. . . . A physical curse may be said to have blasted the spot, where guilt and frenzy consummated the most execrable scene that our history blushes to record. For this was the field where superstition won her darkest triumph; the high place where our fathers set up their shame, to the mournful gaze of generations far remote. The dust of martyrs was beneath our feet.[85]

Despite Hawthorne's evocative description, the summit was probably not the execution site because of the obvious difficulty of transporting the condemned in carts up such a steep hill. The marshal might have made the prisoners get out and walk for the last part of the journey, but that too would have been difficult. George Jacobs was eighty years old and walked with the aid of two sticks. Rebecca Nurse was seventy-one and ill in bed when arrested. Six others of the condemned were aged sixty or over.

Later in Hawthorne's story, he dramatically describes the condemned approaching the gallows:

> Here tottered a woman in her dotage, knowing neither the crime imputed her, nor its punishment; there another, distracted by the universal madness, till fever-

ish dreams were remembered as realities, and she almost believed her guilt. One, a proud man once, was so broken down by the intolerable hatred heaped upon him, that he seemed to hasten his steps, eager to hide himself in the grave hastily dug at the foot of the gallows. . . .[86]

LOCUST TREES OR GALLOWS?

In fact, we do not know if the condemned were hanged from a gallows. The executioner may have used a tree. Contemporary accounts make clear that the prisoners uttered their last words, with nooses around their necks, from ladders. When the ladder was pushed away from whatever it was leaning on, they died a slow, painful death. But whether the ladder was supported by a branch or a scaffold, the sources do not say. There is a tradition that the condemned were hanged from a locust tree. A popular ballad about Giles Cory begins, "Giles Cory was a wizard strong/A stubborn wretch was he/And fit was he to hang on high/Upon the locust tree." But on the spot where the condemned may have hanged trees were not planted until fifty years later. Using a tree might have been cheaper than transporting wood up the hill to construct a gallows, but it would have been hard to hang between five and eight people at once from the branches of one or more trees. The executioner would have had to find enough branches of the right height and strength. And we know that the condemned were all hanged at the same time because, at the executions on September 22, the pastor Nicholas Noyes said, "What a sad thing it is to see eight firebrands of hell hanging there."[87] So it seems likely that they were hanged from a gallows.

Hawthorne's story ends with the telling words, "And here, in dark, funereal stone, should rise another monument, sadly commemorative of the errors of an earlier race, and not to be cast down, while the human heart has one infirmity that may result in crime."[88]

At last, over a hundred and fifty years later, a monument has been built, though not here but next to the Charter Street cemetery—not in dark, funereal stone, but in lighter granite. It commemorates not the errors of the executioners but the integrity and courage of the executed. We could say that it is "not to be cast down, while the human heart has one strength that may result in heroism."

From the summit, take the footpath to the left, leading you downhill to the parking lot. Turn left along Mansell Highway to Proctor Street, where not far along, you will see a rocky ledge between houses, with trees and rough grass. This is Proctor's Ledge, where the locusts once stood.

There were no houses here in 1692. The crowds of spectators could have gathered above and below the gallows. Cotton Mather, who harangued the crowd from his horse after George Burroughs died, saying the devil could disguise himself as "an angel of light,"[89] could have ridden here more easily than to the top of the hill. This peaceful, ordinary spot is far less dramatic to look at than the summit but is more likely to have supported the scaffold and its terrible burden.

Continue down Proctor Street to Boston Road a little farther towards Salem than Hanson Street. Cross the road and walk back to where you started by way of Federal Street, where beautiful eighteenth- and nineteenth-century houses raise the spirits after the troubling experience of visiting the spot where twenty innocent people died.

An office building stands at the corner of St. Peter's and Federal streets, where the Salem Jail stood in 1692. (Ralph Turcotte photo)

The site of old Salem Jail

In 1692, St. Peter's Street was known as Prison Lane, and the jail was at the intersection with Federal Street, where a telephone company building now stands. In the 1930s, a house stood on the site, built with timbers from the jail. In that decade it became Salem's first Witch City attraction, when the Goodall family, who owned it, constructed a replica of the dungeons and charged tourists admission. The Old Witch Jail and Dungeon, as it was known, drew tens of thousands of visitors before being bulldozed to make way for the telephone company building. The attraction then moved to Lynde Street, becoming the "Witch Dungeon," which is still there today. The original timbers from the jail and dungeon were donated to the Peabody Essex Museum but are not on display.

Site of Salem Jail, St. Peter's Street, at the intersection with Federal Street.

❖

The site of Salem meetinghouse

The Salem meetinghouse, where several of the accused witches were interrogated, stood on the spot where the Daniel Low Building now looms, at the corner of Essex and

Washington streets. In 1692, Essex Street was called Main Street and Washington Street was called Town House Street. The buildings on either side of the meetinghouse were large houses belonging to prosperous Salemites. John Hathorne's residence was on the other side of Washington Street, a few yards to the south.

The plaque on the Daniel Low Building reads,

Here stood from 1634 until 1673 the first meetinghouse erected in Salem. No structure was built earlier
for congregational worship by a church formed in
America. It was occupied for secular as well as religious
uses. In it preached, in succession, I. Roger Williams;
II. Hugh Peters; III. Edward Norris; IV. John
Higginson. It was enlarged in 1639 and was last used
for worship in 1670. The first church in Salem, gathered July and August 1629, has had no place of worship
but this spot.

Judging from James Duncan Phillips's map of 1700 Salem, the second meetinghouse, where the examinations were held, was built next to this first one, closer to the corner. John Higginson, an old man in 1692, was still the pastor, although his assistant, Nicholas Noyes, was far more active in the witch hunt. The Daniel Low Building was erected over a hundred years ago as the fourth meetinghouse of the First Church of Salem. That church joined with the North Church in 1923, and the building then ceased to be used as a meetinghouse.

Site of Salem meetinghouse, Essex Street, at the intersection with Washington Street.

The site of Salem courthouse

The building where nineteen men and women were con-
demned to death in 1692 stood in the middle of Washington Street. It was called the Town House, and the lower of its

two floors was used as a school. The trials were conducted
upstairs. The earliest trial was Bridget Bishop's, on June 2. If
the school was still in session, the boys may have been given a
day off. (Only boys, not girls, went to school at that time in
Massachusetts.) Their concentration on their lessons would
have surely been severely disrupted by the screaming and
shouting of the afflicted girls, the booming voice of Judge
Stoughton, and the pleas of the accused.

The marker on the building that is now 70 Washington
Street reads:

> Nearly opposite this spot stood in the middle of the
> street, a building devoted, from 1677 until 1718, to
> municipal and judicial uses. In it, in 1692, were tried
> and condemned for witchcraft most of the nineteen per-
> sons who suffered death on the gallows. Giles Corey
> was here put to trial on the same charge, and, refusing
> to plead, was taken away and pressed to death. In
> January, 1693, twenty-one persons were tried here for
> witchcraft, of whom eighteen were acquitted and three
> condemned, but later set free, together with about 150
> accused persons, in a general delivery which occurred in
> May.

A new courthouse was built, also in the middle of
Washington Street, in 1718. The original building was torn
down in 1760. An engraving from the 1830s shows the
courthouse as it was then. An elegant eighteenth-century
building, it stood near the end of the street, the road running
past it down to the North River. On either side were imposing neoclassical buildings. A hundred and fifty years earlier,
the design would have been much the same, although the
buildings would have lacked spires and turrets and would
have had much smaller windows. The street may have resem-
bled a village green more than a road.

To the left of the Town House stood the residence of the

Salem Trolley at the Burying Point. (Marilyn Haley photo)

minister Nicholas Noyes, highly active in the examinations and trials. He needed to take only a few steps from his front door to the court.

Site of Salem courthouse, Washington Street, opposite no. 70.

The Salem Trolley

For the witch trials tourist, the high point of the Salem trolley ride is when the guide says, "We are now driving through the courthouse." He goes on to explain that the Town House where the alleged witches were tried in 1692 was in the middle of the street. The hour-long ride gives an excellent overview of Salem, from Essex Street to Winter Island. Visitors can alight and reboard at any of the fourteen stops.

The Salem Trolley, based at the Trolley Depot, Essex Street. 978-744-5469. Open daily, April–October; weekends in November.

The Witch House

This is the only house left in Salem with a direct connection to the witch trials. Built in 1675, it was inhabited in 1692 by magistrate Jonathan Corwin and his family. The house was moved thirty-five feet in 1940 to allow the intersection to be widened. It is furnished with original seventeenth-century items, including a four-poster bed, Bible box, and desk. A section of expensive wallpaper such as the Corwins would have had on their walls is on display, as well as implements that stamped butter and waffles with the family seal. Tours by costumed guides include a short talk on the witch trials.

The "Witch House," 310 Essex Street. 978-744-0180. www.salemweb.com. Open daily, May 1–November 30. Admission fee.

Superior Court Building

The Superior Court Building on Washington Street, between Church Street and Federal Street, contains a small collection of relics from the witch trials. Do not be daunted by the austere, guarded entrance and sharp looks from officials. If you explain what your purpose is, they will point the way to the clerks' room, where a glass case contains the 1692 seal of Essex County, used to legalize documents from the witch trials such as death warrants. It also holds pins supposedly used by witches' specters to prick the accusers and reproductions of original witch-trials documents. This collection constitutes all the physical relics from the witch trials on public display. The relics possessed by the Peabody Essex Museum, which include timbers from the Salem prison dungeons, John Proctor's sundial, George Jacobs's two wallking sticks, and a chair once owned by Phillip English, are in storage. So are the Phillips Library's witch trials documents.

Superior Court, Washington Street, between Church Street and Federal Street. Open weekdays 9 A.M.–4.30 P.M.

Phillip English Memorial, St. Peter's Church

On entering St. Peter's Episcopal Church, look to the immediate right of the door. There is a memorial plaque to Phillip English, the rich Salem merchant accused of witchcraft. English avoided trial by escaping from prison. The plaque pays tribute to two early Episcopalians, John Brown and Samuel Brown, and also reads, "In memory of Phillip English who in the year 1733 presented the land on which this edifice is erected. This tablet is inscribed in the year 1833, as a grateful memorial of their devotion to the cause of Christianity, and to the ritual of the Protestant Episcopal Church."

St. Peter's Church, St. Peter's Street. Open Sunday mornings.

Broad Street Cemetery

It is a short walk from the center of Salem to the cemetery on Broad Street, which lies opposite the Pickering House, the oldest residence in America to be continuously occupied by one family. (It is now owned by a foundation set up by members of the Pickering family.) The cemetery ascends the side of a hill, and at the highest point, near a fence, stands a small gray obelisk marking the Corwin family tomb. The faded inscription is hard to read, but among those buried here are Jonathan Corwin, the Salem merchant who was one of the three magistrates at the pretrial examinations of witches, and George Corwin, his twenty-five-year-old nephew who, as sheriff, confiscated the witches' estates. Jonathan Corwin owned the house on Essex Street now known as the Witch House.

Broad Street Cemetery, Broad Street.

Salem History Room in the Salem Public Library

The Salem Public Library is on Essex Street, about fifteen minutes' walk from the Salem Witch Museum, going west. On the top floor is the Salem History Room, where visitors may freely browse through primary sources as well as recent works on the witch trials, including those listed in the Suggested Reading section on page 136. The most useful sources are the original witchcraft documents, including verbatim accounts of examinations, reproduced in *Salem Witchcraft Papers* by Paul Boyer and Stephen Nissenbaum; the several contemporary accounts of the witch hunt reproduced in my *Salem Witch Trials Reader* and George Lincoln Burr's *The Narratives of the Witchcraft Cases;* and the Salem Village church and village records reproduced in Boyer and Nissenbaum's *Salem Village Witchcraft.* Copies of the Essex County Court records are also to be found here.

Salem Public Library, 370 Essex Street. 978-744-0860. Open daily.

The Phillips Library of the Peabody Essex Museum

This houses many of the original witch trials documents. Most are on microfilm and can be consulted by scholars on request. The library also has an extensive collection of books relating to the trials, including those held by the Salem Public Library. Hours open to the public were cut drastically in 2004.

Phillips Library. Essex Street, near the intersection with Hawthorne Boulevard. 800-745-4054. Open Wednesdays 1–5 P.M., Thursdays 1–8 P.M. Admission fee.

The House of the Seven Gables

The historic house's connection to the witch trials is remote but powerful. It is more accurately known as the Turner-Ingersoll Mansion and was built in 1668. Nathaniel

The House of Seven Gables. (Ralph Turcotte photo)

Hawthorne used it as the basis for the house in his novel of the same name. In the first chapter, the character Colonel Pyncheon, based on Hawthorne's great-great-grandfather John Hathorne, dies a mysterious death. The implication is that he has succumbed to the curse of Thomas Maule, hanged for witchcraft, who in the novel declares on the gallows that Pyncheon "shall have blood to drink." Hawthorne was making artistic use of the recorded words of Sarah Good to Nicholas Noyes on July 19, 1692.

A tour of the site also includes a visit to Nathaniel Hawthorne's birthplace, moved here from its original site, and three other houses. A short film on the history of The House of Seven Gables can be viewed in the visitors' entrance hall. The house is owned by The House of Seven Gables Settlement Association.

The House of the Seven Gables, 54 Turner Street. 978-744-0991. www.7gables.org. Open year-round. Admission fee.

⁜

Danvers

It was in Salem Village, not Salem Town, that the witch hunt started, when a group of girls began having hysterical fits and accused three women of witchcraft. The layout of the streets in what was once the center of the Village—Center

Street, Holten Street, Pine Street, and Hobart Street—is the same today as it was in 1692. Visitors can walk from the site of the 1692 meetinghouse, opposite the Danvers Witchcraft Victims' Memorial, to the building that was Ingersoll's tavern and is now a private home, as the Salem Villagers once walked after the examinations of accused witches to drink cider and discuss what they had seen. One can continue on a short distance to the excavated remains of the parsonage, to which Samuel Parris often returned after meeting his friend Nathaniel Ingersoll. Across from the old tavern, one can visit the site of the watch tower, where the men of the village looked out for Indian attacks and where accused witches may have been held.

Visitors should begin a tour at the home of Rebecca Nurse, the fifth woman accused and, after Bridget Bishop, one of the first five to be hanged.

Danvers Historical Society. 978-777-1666.

The Rebecca Nurse Homestead

A dirt road leads out of Pine Street through beautiful pasture and fields to the saltbox-style house where in 1692 the Nurse family lived—Francis, Rebecca, eight children, and several grandchildren. The twenty-seven acres of property are only a small part of the estate that belonged to the house three hundred years ago but are otherwise for the most part unchanged. The owner of the property had rented it to Francis Nurse in 1678, making an arrangement whereby if Francis kept up the payments he would, in twenty years, assume ownership. In modern terms, he gave Francis a mortgage. The Nurses were fortunate; such an arrangement was very unusual at the time. Because Francis had started life humbly and earned a living as a tray maker, he would never have expected to own a three-hundred-acre estate. His and

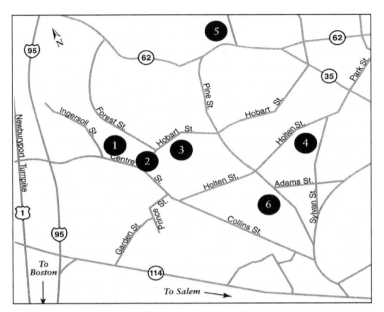

Witch trials sites in present-day Danvers: **1.** *Site of Salem Village parsonage.*
2. *Ingersoll's Ordinary.* **3.** *Witchcraft Victims' Memorial.* **4.** *Danvers Archival*
Center. **5.** *Wadsworth Burial Ground.* **6.** *Rebecca Nurse Homestead.*

Rebecca's good fortune may have aroused the deep envy of
Thomas and Ann Putnam. Both Putnams had been denied
expected inheritances and watched their own fortunes
decline. The Putnams had a further cause for dislike. Both
Francis Nurse and Isaac Towne, Rebecca's father, had been
locked in land disputes with the Putnams for years. When
Ann Putnam the younger and the other hysterical girls began
to accuse respectable women, the second one they named was
Rebecca.

The house has been enlarged since 1692. Though none of
the furniture is original, artifacts in the style of the day give a
strong sense of how those rooms would have looked. Upstairs
is a room containing a bed of the kind Rebecca would have
been lying in when the constable came to arrest her.

Francis Nurse died in 1695, but the house stayed in the
Nurse family until in 1784 it was bought by a Putnam.

However, he was not a descendant of the Nurses' old enemy Thomas Putnam but of his half-brother Joseph. In 1926, the house was bought and restored by the Rebecca Nurse Memorial Association. In 1981, it became the property of the Danvers Alarm List Company, a nonprofit organization.

REPLICA OF SALEM VILLAGE MEETINGHOUSE

On the other side of the driveway from the house stands a replica of the original Salem Village meetinghouse, built for the 1985 film *Three Sovereigns for Sarah,* the story of Sarah Cloyce, Rebecca Nurse's sister, who was also accused of witchcraft but never brought to trial. NightOwl Productions, who made the film, asked Danvers historian Richard Trask to research the Salem Village meetinghouse, long since gone, so they could build as authentic a replica as possible. Mr. Trask used the original records of Massachusetts's three surviving meetinghouses and closely examined the structures that remain in order to make educated guesses about the form and appearance of the original Salem Village meetinghouse. Its dimensions were never in doubt since the village record book for November 1672 states that the building would be thirty-four by twenty-eight feet, with sixteen feet between joints.

The meetinghouse is unadorned, inside and out. The Puritans believed artworks, religious or secular, were sinful distractions. The building was unheated and in the winter got so bitterly cold that the congregation would wrap themselves in blankets and settle foot warmers and dogs on their feet. Men and women sat separately, on opposite sides of the aisle, with children, slaves, and servants in the galleries. The seating order reflected the Salem Village social hierarchy, with the most prosperous villagers at the front. At the two Sunday services, of three hours in the morning, two in the afternoon, the only music was the unaccompanied singing of psalms. There followed a prayer and a long, repetitive, often terrifying sermon. Pastor Samuel Parris, the father of one of the girls who first went into hysterics and started making witchcraft accusations, stood in the pulpit and declaimed words such as, "Oh Sinners! Time enough, time enough, have but a little patience, and you shall see an hell time enough, wrath will overtake you time enough, if you prevent it not by true repentance."[90] On March 27, 1692, he preached a sermon he described as "occasioned by dreadful witchcraft broke out here a few weeks past, and one member of this church, and another of Salem upon public examination by civil authority vehemently suspected for she-witches, and upon it committed."[91] The text of the sermon was "Have I not chosen you twelve, and one of you is a devil." He helped drive on the witch hunt by implying he believed Martha Cory and Rebecca Nurse were guilty. When Parris said what his text was, Rebecca Nurse's sister Sarah Cloyce left the meetinghouse, slamming the door. Shortly afterwards, she too was accused.

Following the completion of *Three Sovereigns for Sarah*, the reconstructed meetinghouse was donated to the Nurse Homestead. In the summer, sound and light shows, lasting twenty-five minutes, depict the story of the beginnings of the witch hunt. Particularly effective are recreations of the services and examinations in this replica of their original setting. In 1692, the Salem Village meetinghouse was of course not here but on Hobart Street, opposite where the Witchcraft Victims' Memorial now stands.

NURSE FAMILY CEMETERY

A short walk along a path down the hill takes you to the Nurse family cemetery and its imposing memorial to Rebecca Nurse. Erected in 1885, this granite monument was dedicated in a ceremony attended by six hundred people after a service in the meetinghouse. The poem on the front was

Memorial to Rebecca Nurse in the Nurse family cemetery. (Ralph Turcotte photo)

specially composed by Amesbury poet and abolitionist John Greenleaf Whittier:

> Oh Christian Martyr! Who for Truth could die
> When all about thee owned the hideous lie!
> The world, redeemed from superstition's sway,
> Is breathing freer for thy sake today.

Nearby is the grave where the probable remains of George Jacobs were buried in 1992. The bones were dug up on the Jacobs farm in the mid-nineteenth century, reburied, and then in the 1950s dug up again and entrusted to the Danvers Alarm List Company. The company kept them in storage until they buried them here.

Tradition has it that the bodies of both George Jacobs and Rebecca Nurse were removed from Gallows Hill by their families after dark, to be buried on their own land. The remains of Rebecca Nurse may well be in an unknown grave somewhere on the property.

To reach the homestead, travel north on Route 128, take Exit 24, turn right onto Endicott Street, and right on Sylvan Street, and then bear left to Pine Street.

The Nurse Homestead, 149 Pine Street. 978-774-8799. Open summer and early fall. Admission fee.

The Site of the Salem Village Parsonage

Tucked behind the houses of Center Street, down a path between numbers 67 and 69, is the excavated site of the parsonage where the witch hunt began. Here, Betty Parris and Abigail Williams went into fits and accused Tituba, Sarah Good, and Sarah Osborne of witchcraft. The house was built in 1681, pulled down in 1784, and excavated in 1970. The house's foundations are visible, and excellent signs give archaeological and historical information.

Parsonage site, pathway between 67 and 69 Center Street.

Salem Village Training Field

Near the site of the parsonage, off Center Street, is a field first used for training by the Salem Village militia in 1671. A marker erected by the Danvers Historical Commission in 1974 reads, "Defense was a prime necessity to the settlers of Salem Village, and as early as 1671 the male inhabitants began meeting here for military drill. This preparation was heightened in 1675 during the King Philip's War in which many villagers took part. In 1709 Deacon Nathaniel Ingersoll willed this field to the inhabitants of Salem Village for a training place forever."

Salem Village Training Field, Center Street.

Ingersoll's Ordinary

In Puritan New England, the word *ordinary* meant tavern. The earliest portion of this building, at the intersection of Hobart and Center streets, was built around 1670. In 1692, it was owned by Nathaniel Ingersoll, a close friend and associate of Samuel Parris and Thomas Putnam. The tavern was one of the two centers of Salem Village life. The other was the meetinghouse. It was at Ingersoll's that the villagers

*Ingersoll's Ordinary
(Ralph Turcotte
photo)*

gathered for cider and cakes between services on Sundays and, in the months from March to September 1692, after the examinations of witches. The villagers' enthusiasm for the tavern may seem surprising, but in Puritan Massachusetts moderate drinking was regarded as normal. Cider and ale were taken with family meals. The witch hunt meant good business for Nathaniel Ingersoll. A bill run up on March 1, the first day of the examinations of Tituba, Sarah Good, and Sarah Osborne, shows the marshals, constables, and assistants spending three shillings on food and two shillings on cider. The constables laid out an extra ninepence on cider and sixpence on rum.

The building is now a private house.

Ingersoll's Ordinary, 199 Hobart Street, at the intersection with Center Street. Not open to the public.

Site of the Salem Village watch tower

In 1692, almost opposite Ingersoll's tavern at the highest elevation of the village, where today stands a church, was a watch tower. It was a two-story wooden building manned by members of the local militia on the lookout for Indians. Some of the alleged witches may have been briefly imprisoned here before being taken to Salem. The hill was higher then, so the watch tower had a wide view over forests and fields, perhaps as far as to the sea. In 1702, it was knocked down, the hill graded and a new meetinghouse built. The old one on Hobart Street, where the examinations took place, was abandoned. In the new building, in 1706, Ann Putnam made her apology, read aloud by the pastor Joseph Green, for "the accusing of several persons of a grievous crime, whereby their lives were taken away from them."[92]

A marker erected by the Massachusetts Bay Colony Tercentenary Commission in 1930 reads, "The Church in Salem Village. To this church, rent by the witchcraft frenzy, came in 1697 the Reverend Joseph Green, aged twenty-two. He induced the mischief makers to confess, reconciled the factions, established the first public school and became noted for his skill at hunting game and his generous hospitality." It was not of course in the modern building standing here now that Joseph Green preached but in the meetinghouse built in 1702, long since gone.

First Church, intersection of Hobart and Center streets.

Witchcraft Victims' Memorial

The memorial stands on Hobart Street, directly opposite the site of the original Salem Village meetinghouse. The granite block in front of the three-panelled wall, topped by a stone replica of an oversized Bible box, is directly aligned with the original meetinghouse pulpit. Resting on the Bible box is an open book sculpted in stone, inscribed "THE BOOK OF LIFE." Together with the engraving of a figure on the top of the wall, who could represent either a pastor or magistrate, these artifacts bring to mind the examinations held in the meetinghouse opposite.

The rosettes on the front of the Bible box are Puritan design features found on furniture and gravestones of the

Witchcraft Victims' Memorial, Danvers (Photo by Richard B. Trask)

same period. The five rosettes banded together by a serpentine vine are symbols of eternity. The shackles, broken in two by the book, represent the chains of falsehood smashed asunder by truth. Carved on the face of the block are the words, "In memory of those innocents who died during the Salem village witchcraft hysteria of 1692."

The central panel of the granite wall behind the block gives the names of the twenty-five innocent victims and the dates when they died. They include not only the nineteen who were hanged and the one pressed to death but also the five who died in jail. On each side of the panel stands a wall at a 45-degree angle, inscribed with statements made by eight of the victims, either during their examinations or in prison. The designers of the memorial were Richard B. Trask, Robert O. Farley, and Marjorie C. Weitzel. It was dedicated before an audience of over three thousand people on May 9, 1992.

Danvers Witchcraft Victims' Memorial, 176 Hobart Street. Open dawn to dusk.

Sarah Holten House

The house that was inhabited by Sarah Holten, who testified against Rebecca Nurse in 1692, stands at the corner of Center Street and Holten Street. The Holtens' land was adjacent to the Nurses'. In a deposition to the court Sarah Holten claimed that three years before Rebecca Nurse ". . . came to our house and fell a railing at [Sarah's husband] because our pigs got into her field . . . and within a short time after this my poor husband . . . was taken with a strange fit . . . [and] he departed this life by a cruel death."[93]

Sarah's was one of only three depositions accusing Rebecca of witchcraft, apart from those of the afflicted girls, Thomas Putnam and several other Putnams, Samuel Parris, and the Ingersolls. Nathaniel and Hannah Ingersoll supported Sarah Holten's story, saying, "We were conversant with Benjamin Holten for above a week before he died and he was acted in a very strange manner with most violent fits, acting much like to our poor bewitched persons when we thought they would have died."[94]

Yet Sarah Holten signed the petition gathered for Rebecca, which said that those whose names "are hereunto subscribed" were testifying that they had known her for many years and never had any grounds to suspect her of "any such thing as she is now accused of," that is, witchcraft.[95] The inconsistency in Sarah's behavior may be attributed to her confusion of mind in those most confusing times.

The house was built about 1660. It is now owned by the Daughters of the American Revolution.

Sarah Holten House, 177 Holten Street. 978-777-6084. Open by appointment.

Joseph Holten House

Next to the Sarah Holten House is the house Joseph Holten lived in, built about 1671. He also signed the petition supporting Rebecca Nurse. It is now privately owned.

Joseph Holten House, 19 Center Street. Not open to the public.

Thomas Haines House

At 35 Center Street, near the church, is the house that was Thomas Haines's, built in 1681. Haines gave testimony that helped send Elizabeth Howe of Topsfield to the gallows. He also testified, with Nathaniel Ingersoll, that Abigail Hobbs had said that her father William would leave the house when the Bible was read. It is in private hands.

Thomas Haines House, 35 Center Street. Not open to public.

Wadsworth Burial Ground

This is the ancient Salem Village burial ground, dating from the 1640s. Elizabeth Parris, wife of Samuel Parris, was buried here in 1696, aged "about 48 years." To find her grave, follow the path straight ahead from the entrance on Summer Street to where it turns left. The stone is in the corner plot. The inscription is almost illegible now, with the last line of the verse, composed by Samuel Parris, only just above the ground. The verse reads:

> Sleep precious Dust no Stranger now to Rest.
> Thou hast thy longed wish in Abrahams Brest.
> Farewell best Wife, choice Mother, Neighbor, Friend.
> Weel wail the less for hopes of Thee I th End.

If it seems surprising that Samuel Parris should turn his hand to composing verse, remember that he would have thought of himself as a writer, penning elaborate sermons, full of rhetorical devices and figures of speech, week after week.

Entrance to Wadsworth Burial Ground. (Ralph Turcotte photo)

Nearer the Summer Street entrance is a new stone inscribed to John Putnam, 1580–1662, and Captain John Putnam, 1627–1710. The stone says, "In this plot rest the remains of immigrants from Aston Abbots, co. Bucks, England, 1640." John Putnam was the first of the clan to settle in Salem Village. Captain John Putnam was his third son. He and his wife Rebecca were the couple who gave house room to the Reverend George Burroughs and his wife in 1681 while the parsonage was under construction. Two years later Captain John had the minister arrested for debt, but he later dropped the charges. The debt was for funeral expenses for Burroughs's first wife, who had died the previous year. She also lies in this cemetery, in an unmarked grave, as does Burroughs's second wife, who died in 1683. This second wife was Sarah Ruck Hathorne, the widow of John Hathorne's brother. In 1692, Ann Putnam claimed she had seen the ghosts of both wives and declared Rev. Burroughs had murdered them.

Wadsworth Burial Ground, 18 Summer Street.

117

Sarah Osborne House

This house was built about 1660 and inhabited in 1692 by Sarah Osborne, one of the first three women to be accused of witchcraft. It was moved here from its original site in 1914.

Sarah Osborne House, 272 Maple Street, opposite Gorman Road. Not open to the public.

Joseph Putnam House

The original house on this spot was bequeathed to Joseph Putnam by his father Thomas Putnam Senior in 1686. Together with the house went the ample family homestead and many of the most fertile acres granted to John Putnam, the original settler, forty years before. This unusual bequest may have set off the witch hunt. Joseph was Thomas's youngest son, his only child by his second wife. In Puritan New England, as in Old England, it was usual for a father to leave the family estate to the eldest son. Thomas's eldest was Thomas Putnam Junior, father of the afflicted Ann Putnam. So, when Thomas Senior left the homestead to Joseph, he deprived Thomas of his expected inheritance. Thomas Junior contested the wills of both his father and, later, his stepmother. Bitterness and resentment over his failure in these lawsuits may have helped induce him to encourage his twelve-year-old daughter Ann Putnam to name people he hated or envied as witches.

Joseph Putnam House. (Ralph Turcotte photo)

But Ann never named the person Thomas may have hated and envied most of all, his half brother Joseph, possibly because of fear of the consequences. Joseph made it clear that he would kill anyone who tried to arrest him. During the time of the witch hunt he kept a horse saddled day and night, claiming that if the marshal came with forces he would leap into the saddle, fighting off anyone who chased him.

The present house has been considerably altered over the years and retains little or none of the structure that stood in 1692. It is owned by the Danvers Historical Society.

Joseph Putnam House, 431 Maple Street, at the southeast portion of the cloverleaf intersection of Route 1 and Route 62. 978-777-1666. Open by appointment.

The Putnam Cemetery (Private)

Near the Joseph Putnam House, on what was once the Putnam homestead, is the burial ground where lie Thomas Putnam, his wife Ann Putnam, and their daughter Ann Putnam.

The Putnam Cemetery, Route 62, just west of its intersection with Route 1. Not open to public.

The Danvers Archival Center

The center is part of the Peabody Institute Library in Danvers. The department houses an extensive collection of town records, including the Salem Village Church Book of Record. Other manuscript materials include journals, diaries, deeds, wills, and inventories. The center also houses printed matter relating to the witchcraft hysteria, including copies of rare volumes such as Cotton Mather's *Wonders of the Invisible World* and Robert Calef's *More Wonders of the Invisible World*. A section of the archives relating to local history includes biographies of Samuel Parris and Israel Putnam. Manuscripts

Bridget Bishop House. (Ralph Turcotte photo)

and rare books are kept in a climate-controlled storage area. They are accessible to researchers by appointment. Other items are on the public shelves of the reading room. The center is headed by Richard Trask, Danvers's leading local historian and author of *The Devil Hath Been Raised.*

Danvers Archival Center, 15 Sylvan Street. 978-774-0554. Open limited hours on weekdays and Saturdays.

Bridget Bishop House

The house referred to in all older guidebooks as the Bridget Bishop House was in fact owned by Sarah Bishop, accused of witchcraft and imprisoned but never brought to trial. Bridget Bishop was the first accused witch to be hanged. The confusion between Bridget and Sarah goes all the way back to 1692. The Beverly minister John Hale made a long deposition against a "Goodwife Bishop" married to Edward Bishop, saying she kept an unruly house where people drank and played "shovel-board" at "unseasonable hours in the night."[96] He never gave "Goodwife Bishop's" first name. Both Bridget and Sarah were married to husbands named Edward, the main source of the confusion. Hale's deposition was mistakenly filed early on with Bridget Bishop's papers. Charles W. Upham, writing in the 1800s in *Salem Witchcraft,* understandably assumed the Goodwife Bishop that Hale referred to was Bridget. He depicted her in his book as an unconventional character who posed a moral and sexual threat to the strict

Puritan community. But it was Sarah, not Bridget, who lived
in this house on the border of Salem Village and Beverly and
used it as a tavern. Both she and her husband were accused
of witchcraft and imprisoned. Her husband was targeted
after he had cured John Indian of a "fit" by hitting him with
a stick and then declaring he did not doubt he could cure all
the afflicted by similar means.

*Bridget (Sarah) Bishop House, 238 Conant Street. Not open to
the public.*

Peabody

In Peabody, visitors will find four sites connected with the
witch trials. For more information, contact the Peabody
Historical Society at 978-531-0805.

John Proctor House

The present house is on the spot where John Proctor lived in
1692, but it was not built until the early eighteenth century.
The original house burned down. Driving along Lowell
Street from Salem, the house is on the left after the intersection with Route 128.

John Proctor House, 348 Lowell Street. Not open to the public.

Giles Cory's Farm

An abandoned twentieth-century house now stands on the
site of Giles Cory's house on Pine Street, West Peabody. To
reach the spot from Salem, take Boston Street to Lowell
Street, pass under Routes 128 and 95, turn left along Lake
Street and left again onto Pine Street. The abandoned house
is on the corner.

Giles Cory's farm, Pine Street, West Peabody.

Memorial to Giles and Martha Cory

In 1992 a memorial was erected to Giles and Martha Cory. It takes the form of two adjacent granite headstones, one inscribed, "WITCH HYSTERIA MARTYR, IRASCIBLE UNYIELD-ING GILES COREY DIED UNDER THE TORTURE OF STONE WEIGHTS SEPTEMBER 19, 1692," the other, "WITCH HYSTERIA MARTYR, PIOUS OUTSPOKEN MARTHA COREY HANGED SEP-TEMBER 22, 1692." It can be found by going west on Lowell Street to the point on the left where the railroad tracks pass between the two parts of Crystal Lake. The site of the memorial was part of the Cory farm in 1692.

Memorial to Giles and Martha Cory, Lowell Street

Nathaniel Felton House

Built about 1644, this house was inhabited by Nathaniel Felton, who signed a petition, with several other neighbors, on behalf of John and Elizabeth Proctor. The petition said the signatories had no reason to think of the Proctors as guilty of the witchcraft crimes they were accused of and had known them always to live "Christian-like." The original document is in the Phillips Library of the Peabody Essex Museum. The Peabody Historical Society has a copy. The house is the oldest in Peabody and is owned by the Historical Society. To reach it from Salem, take Boston Street to Lowell Street, pass under Routes 128 and 95, turn right on Prospect Street and left onto Felton Street. The house is at the end of the road.

Nathaniel Felton House, Felton Street. 978-531-0805. Open by appointment.

Hale Farm. (Courtesy of the Beverly Historical Society and Museum, Beverly, Mass.)

Beverly

Just over the bridge from Salem, Beverly offers three interesting sites to visit. For more information, contact the Beverly Historical Society at 978-922-1186. (www.beverlyhistory.org)

⟡

John Hale House

The oldest part of this beautiful house was built in about 1694 by the Reverend John Hale, the Beverly minister who played an active part in the witch hunt. It was originally a saltbox design, two rooms up, two down, with a central chimney. Hale wrote his book on the witch trials, *A Modest Enquiry into the Nature of Witchcraft,* in his study in this house. He lived here until his death in 1700. During his lifetime, the house was the only one in the area and the property extended down to the seashore. It was owned and enlarged by Hale descendants over the next two hundred years. Since 1937 it has been in the possession of the Beverly Historical Society. Though usually referred to as the Hale House, its correct name is Hale Farm.

Hale Farm, 39 Hale Street. 978-922-1186. Open by appointment.

Ancient Burial Ground

The burial ground is near Hale Farm, on what was once the Hale property. Within a walled area are the Hale family graves. John Hale's is on the left, its beautiful decorations, including a death's head with upswept wings, still quite visible. To its right is the grave containing the remains of both Hale's wives, Rebecca and Sarah. Rebecca died in 1683. Her daughter also lies here. Hale's second wife, Sarah, was accused of witchcraft in 1692, causing Hale to reverse his opinion of the witch hunt. She died in 1697.

Ancient Burial Ground, 15 Abbott Street, behind fire station.

Beverly Historical Society

The Historical Society contains a rare first edition of the Reverend John Hale's *A Modest Enquiry into the Nature of Witchcraft* and a halberd, or staff of office, used by the Beverly constable during the witch trials. He would have carried it when escorting prisoners to examinations, trials, or prison.

Beverly Historical Society, 117 Cabot Street. 978-922-1186.

North Andover

In 1692, this area north of Salem Village, was known simply as Andover. The area called Andover today and what is now North Andover were one. The witch hunt spread to the region in July 1692 when Joseph Ballard summoned the afflicted girls to discover who was bewitching his wife. Eventually Andover had its own band of afflicted girls, and more people were accused and imprisoned from there than from any other area. The region that was once the village center has preserved its rural character. The focal point is the ancient burying ground, nestled among fields in a hollow. The original meetinghouse stood next to it, but there are no remains of this structure today. Slightly up the hill, on Osgood Street, is the house built for the Reverend Thomas Barnard in 1711.

For more information, contact the North Andover Historical Society at 978-686-4035 and the Andover Historical Society at 978-475-2236.

The Burying Ground

The Burying Ground contains a number of graves of people associated with the witch hunt.

William Barker Senior, forty-seven, was arrested in August for having "woefully afflicted and abused" two of the "afflicted girls" of Andover.[97] At his examination he may have expressed deep longings when he said that the devil had promised to "pay all his debts and he should live comfortably" and also that "the devil promised that all his people should live bravely, that all persons should be equal; that there should be no day of resurrection or judgement; and neither punishment nor shame for sin."[98] He escaped from prison soon after being examined and was never brought to trial. He died in 1718.

William Barker Junior (died 1745) was fourteen years old when arrested for bewitching the Andover girls. He was examined and imprisoned but released on bail in October and found not guilty on May 10, 1693.

Timothy Swan (died 1693, age thirty) was the only person in Andover or Salem Village who was afflicted in the sense of suffering from a physical illness. He was probably bedridden from August 1692 and died in January 1693. He was one of the accusers at the "Andover touch test" on September 7, when eighteen people were arrested and imprisoned.

Capt. Timothy Johnson (died 1771) was the son of Rebecca Johnson, who, with her daughter, was accused of

Old Burying Ground. (Ralph Turcotte photo)

witchcraft in 1692. At her examination in January 1693, she acknowledged using a fortune-telling method similar to a ouija board to find out if her brother-in-law, who had been captured by Indians, was alive. She said the Reverend Thomas Barnard told her daughter the words to use to make the method work.

The Reverend Thomas Barnard (died 1718) is also buried in this graveyard. In early September 1692 he was an enthusiastic witch hunter, organizing the "Andover touch test." But on October 18 he signed a petition on behalf of the accused witches. It seems possible his change of heart may have been brought about partly by the discovery that he himself was implicated in supernatural activities. He remained the minister in Andover until his death. His house at 179 Osgood Street, built in 1711, can be seen from the burying ground.

Capt. Christopher Osgood (died 1723) was the father of one of the Andover accused, Mary Osgood Marston. Martha Carrier, the first person from Andover to be arrested as a witch and one of the only three to be executed, had been accused of murdering Osgood's wife and child.

Moses Tyler (died 1727) was the stepfather of the most prominent of the Andover girls, Martha Sprague. Martha, her mother, and five brothers and sisters lived with Moses and his ten sons on the Andover and Boxford town line.

Old Burying Ground, Academy Road, one-tenth of a mile from its intersection with Main Street in North Andover.

Thomas Barnard House

This house was built for the Reverend Thomas Barnard in 1711 and, after his death in 1718, was inhabited by his son John Barnard.

Thomas Barnard House, 179 Osgood Street. 978-686-4035. Open May–September.

The Barker Homestead

The Barker homestead, where William Barker Senior and William Barker Junior were arrested in 1692, is still inhabited by the Barker family, though none of the original buildings remain. Visitors can buy produce from a vegetable stand on the property on Route 125, north of Osgood Street, well marked by a sign reading "The Barker Farm."

The Barker Homestead, Route 125, North Andover.

Benjamin Abbott House

Built about 1689, this house was inhabited by Benjamin Abbott, who accused Martha Carrier, hanged as a witch in 1692, of bewitching him so that he broke out in sores on his groin.

Benjamin Abbott House, 9 Andover Street, off Central Street, Andover. Privately owned.

Chandler Bixby House

This dwelling was built sometime between 1674 and 1688 by Thomas Chandler for his daughter Hannah, as a wedding gift after her marriage to Daniel Bixby. The whole family became accusers in the Andover witch hunt. A second daughter of Thomas Chandler's, twelve-year-old Phoebe Chandler, testified against Martha Carrier, saying that she had made her go deaf, and against Richard Carrier, saying that when he looked at her in the meetinghouse she felt a pain in her shoulder.

Chandler Bixby House, 88 Lowell Street (Route 133), Andover. Privately owned.

Topsfield

In Topsfield, two sites of interest commemorate the witch trials. For more information, contact the Topsfield Historical Society at 978-887-3998.

The Capen House

Opposite the Congregational Church of Topsfield, at the northeastern corner of the common, is the house inhabited in 1692 by Pastor Joseph Capen. He was an opponent of the witch hunt. Mary Easty and Sarah Cloyce of Topsfield, the sisters of the executed witch Rebecca Nurse, petitioned the Court of Oyer and Terminer from prison to allow those who knew them best, including Pastor Capen, to speak for them at their trial. The petition was ignored. Mary Easty was convicted and hanged, but Sarah Cloyce was never tried and was eventually released. The house is the original seventeenth-century building, carefully restored.

The Capen House, Howlett Street. 978-887-3998. Open Wednesdays, Fridays, and Sundays, 1–4:30 P.M., mid-June to mid-September.

Topsfield Marker

The Topsfield Historical Society placed a stone marker on the common in 1992 inscribed, "In the memory of three women of Topsfield Parish, Mary Easty, Elizabeth How, Sarah Wildes, Victims of The Witchcraft Delusion of 1692."

Marblehead

Worth the visit for its charm alone, Marblehead also offers the fascinating Old Burial Hill. For more information, contact the Marblehead Historical Society at 781-631-1768.

Old Burial Hill and Redd's Pond

Wilmott Redd of Marblehead, hanged for witchcraft in 1692, lived in a house at the base of Old Burial Hill, somewhere alongside the pond now called Redd's Pond. A sign on the Pond Street side of the water describes her as "Mammy Redd, a fishwife." The wife of Ambrose Gale, who testified that Wilmott Redd had cursed a Mrs. Syms with constipation, is buried in this graveyard. To reach the burial ground and pond from Salem take Route 114, which becomes Pleasant Street, to the end, and then turn left onto Orne Street. At the top of the hill you will find Old Burial Hill.

Old Burial Hill, Orne Street.

Ambrose Gale House

Built around 1663, this large house, with gray wooden slats and a blue front door, belonged in 1692 to Ambrose Gale, who testified that Wilmott Redd had cursed a Mrs. Syms with "dry belly ache" or constipation.

Ambrose Gale House, 17 Franklin Street, between Washington and Selman streets. Privately owned.

Wenham

❖

Claflin-Gerrish-Richards House

This 1662–73 house is part of the Wenham Historical Association and Museum on Main Street. The Reverend Joseph Gerrish lived here in 1692, and it was here that Mary Herrick told him and the Reverend John Hale that the specter of Hale's wife had afflicted her.

Claflin-Gerrish-Richards House, Main Street, opposite the intersection with Monument Street. 978-468-2377. Open year-round except for major holidays. Closed Mondays. Tours of the house are available daily.

❖

Solart–Woodward House

This is the house Sarah Good's father, John Solart, built in 1670 when she was seventeen. He was a prosperous man and ran an inn here. Sarah fell on hard times when she married the itinerant worker William Good and moved to Salem Village. By the time she was accused of witchcraft in 1692, she had been reduced to begging from door to door.

Solart-Woodward House, 106 Main Street, a short distance north of Wenham Burying Ground. Privately owned.

❖

Old Wenham Burying Ground

Three men associated with the witch trials are buried here: Joseph Gerrish, minister of the First Church of Wenham; Thomas Fisk, the son of the Court of Oyer and Terminer jury foreman; and William Fisk, another member of the same jury, who signed the 1697 apology.

Old Wenham Burying Ground, Main Street, Wenham

Amesbury

⚜

Susannah Martin Marker

At the end of North Martin Road, a small boulder with a bronze plaque has been set, marking the site of Susannah Martin's homestead. Of all the women hanged as witches in 1692, Susannah lived farthest from Salem Village. In her examination, she showed herself a highly brave and intelligent woman, unafraid of expressing skepticism about the accusers' fits. The marker describes Susannah as "an honest, hard working Christian woman." When the highway was built, the marker was moved from its former place on what was then Martin Street.

Susannah Martin marker, North Martin Street.

Newbury

⚜

John Atkinson House

It was in this enchanting First Period house, built in 1664–1665, that Sarah Atkinson claimed to have witnessed

John Atkinson House. (Ralph Turcotte photo)

Susannah Martin arriving bone dry out of a storm. She testified in 1692 that "sometimes in the spring of the year about eighteen years since, an extraordinary dirty season when it was not fit for any person to travel, she then came on foot . . . she was as dry as I was . . . I was startled at it that she should come so dry and told her that I should have been wet up to my knees if I should have come so far on foot."[99]

The house, once again owned by the Atkinson family, stands on the Upper Green in Newbury. Traveling north on Route 1A, turn left at the lights. There is a sign on the fence.

John Atkinson House, Upper Green. Privately owned.

Boston

About twenty miles from Salem, Boston has three intriguing burial grounds relevant to the witch trials.

King's Chapel Burying Ground

This is Boston's oldest burying place. Interred here are Thomas Brattle, whose famous letter helped bring the witch hunt to an end, and Maj. Gen. Wait Still Winthrop, who sat as a judge on the Court of Oyer and Terminer and later the Superior Court.

The cemetery is on Tremont Street, next to King's Chapel. A site map with accompanying index can be viewed at the Bostonian Society Library at 15 State Street.

King's Chapel Burying Ground, Tremont Street. 617-635-4505 ext. 6516. Open daylight hours.

Granary Burying Ground

The minister and judge Samuel Sewall, who served on the Court of Oyer and Terminer, is buried in the Granary Burying Ground, in the northwest portion of the cemetery.

Granary Burying Ground, Tremont Street. 617-635-4505 ext. 6516. Open daylight hours.

The Mather tomb in Copp's Hill Burying Ground. (Ralph Turcotte photo)

Copp's Hill Burying Ground

Following the main path to the end of Copp's Hill burying ground, you reach the Mather Tomb. Increase and Cotton Mather are buried here.

Copp's Hill Burying Ground, between Hull Street and Charter Street, North End. 617-635-4505 ext. 6516. Open daylight hours.

GLOSSARY

❖

COMPLAINT: A legal procedure whereby one or more people informed the magistrates of an injury they believed should lead to an arrest. It also referred to the official complaint document issued by the authorities, giving details of the alleged perpetrators, victims, and offences.

COURT OF OYER AND TERMINER: An ad hoc court set up in May 1692 by the new governor, Sir William Phips, specifically to try accused witches. Whether it was legal and proper in the Massachusetts colony at the time has never been resolved. The court sat for the first time on June 2, 1692, to try Bridget Bishop. William Stoughton, the chief judge, presided, as he did at all the subsequent trials. The court was formally dissolved on October 29, after condemning nineteen people to be hanged and one pressed to death.

CRY OUT ON: To name as a witch. "Abigail cried out on Tituba," means "Abigail said Tituba was bewitching her."

EXAMINATION: The pretrial interrogation of alleged witches by the magistrates, to determine whether there was enough evidence to warrant a trial. In only one case out of nearly two hundred did the magistrates find that there was not enough evidence. The lucky suspect was Nehemiah Abbott, a Topsfield weaver. The accusing girls faltered in their insistence that he had bewitched them and finally admitted that the guilty party had a wart on his nose, wheras Abbott did not.

FAMILIAR: A small animal or imp, which supposedly suckled on a "witch's teat" somewhere on the witch's body. The creature was thought to assist in the alleged witchcraft.

MEETINGHOUSE: The building used for Puritan church services and other community activities, such as town meetings.

PURITANS: Originally, a group within the Church of England that espoused the theological doctrines of John Calvin and aimed to "purify" the English church. Some members wished to break away from the Church of England completely. A group of these, known as Separatists, arrived at Plymouth Rock in 1620 and founded Plymouth Colony. Others, the Congregationalists, wanted to reform the Anglican Church rather than separate from it, and a group of them arrived in Salem ten years later to found the Massachusetts Bay Colony. Only those who demonstrated convincingly by oral testimony that they had found God's grace were allowed to take communion. By law, everyone who lived in the Massachusetts Bay Colony had to attend Puritan church services; no other faiths were allowed.

SPECTER: The spirit of a living person. Controlled by its owner and possessing physical powers, it was thought capable of inflicting harm in the same way as a human could. The specter, or "shape," as it was also known, was sent out by a witch to harm his or her victims. It was thought to be capable of traveling long distances, flying through the air.

SPECTRAL EVIDENCE: Testimony by the afflicted girls that they saw witches' specters doing harm to them or to others.

TOUCH TEST: A method of examining witches, wherein an accuser touched an accused. If the accuser claimed to feel better, this was believed to prove witchcraft had flowed from the bewitched girl back to the witch.

SUGGESTED READING

❖

Hill, Frances. *A Delusion of Satan: The Full Story of the Salem Witch Trials, 2nd ed.* New York: Da Capo Press, 2002. An accurate, inclusive, up-to-date, and very readable introduction to the witch trials.

Hill, Frances. *The Salem Witch Trials Reader.* New York: Da Capo Press, 2000. Includes many contemporary records, bringing alive the people and events through personal accounts. Gives an overview of the background to the trials, later historians' accounts and the use of the trials in fiction.

Hill, Frances. *Such Men Are Dangerous: The Fanatics of 1692 and 2004.* Hinesburg, Vt.: Upper Access Inc., 2004. A compelling comparison of the Puritan Massachusetts leaders of 1692 with the Bush administration.

Boyer, Paul and Stephen Nissenbaum. *Salem Possessed.* Cambridge: Harvard University Press, 1974. A seminal work that established the socioeconomic and political factors that brought about the witch hunt. Fascinating reading.

Hoffer, Peter Charles. *The Salem Witchcraft Trials, A Legal History.* Lawrence, Kan.: University Press of Kansas, 1997. A good account for people particularly interested in the legal aspects of the witch trials.

Robinson, Enders. *The Devil Discovered.* New York: Waveland Publications, 1991. Shows how different vested interests worked together to target their victims. Most illuminating, though sometimes oversimplified.

Rosenthal, Bernard. *Salem Story, Reading the Witch Trials of 1692.* Cambridge: Cambridge University Press, 1993. Fascinating reading for anyone who already knows the story well and wants to delve deeper. Reading the trial records and evidence with precision and insight, Rosenthal gives illuminating answers to questions such as "hysteria or fraud?" and "Why the persecution of George Burroughs?"

Upham, Charles W. *Salem Witchcraft.* Boston: Dover Press, 1867. A magisterial two-volume tome that is in some ways misleading but gives a thorough account of the local political background to the witch hunt.

Trask, Richard B. *The Devil Hath Been Raised.* West Kennebunk, Me.: Phoenix Publishing, 1992. Consists of contemporary texts describing the start of the witch hunt, short biographies of key participants, and an essay on the demographics of Salem Village.

Roach, Marilynne K. *The Salem Witch Trials: A Day to Day Chronicle of a Community under Siege.* New York: Cooper Square Publishers, 2002. A fascinating account of events leading up to, during, and following the witch trials.

Roach, Marilynne K. *Gallows and Graves: The Search to Locate the Death and Burial Sites of the People Executed for Witchcraft in 1692.* Watertown, Mass.: Sassafras Grove Press, 1997. An excellent booklet that explains the different theories of the 1692 gallows sites. Includes useful maps.

Bouchard, Betty J. *Our Silent Neighbours: A Study of Gravestones in the Old Salem Area.* Salem: TBS Enterprises, 1991. An excellent guide, with pictures and maps, to the cemeteries of the Salem area.

USEFUL WEB SITES:
   www.franceshill.net
   http://etext.lib.virginia.edu/salem/witchcraft
   www.salemwitchmuseum.com
   www.salemweb.com
   www.rebeccanurse.org

NOTES

❖

1. Frances Hill, *The Salem Witch Trials Reader,* (New York: Da Capo Press, 2000), 59.
2. George Lincoln Burr, *Narratives of the Witchcraft Cases,* (New York: Scribner's, 1914), 341–342.
3. Hill, 59.
4. Ibid., 123.
5. Paul Boyer and Stephen Nissenbaum, *Salem Witchcraft Papers,* (New York: Da Capo Press, 1977), 665.
6. Richard B. Trask, *The Devil Hath Been Raised,* (West Kennebunk: Phoenix Publishing, 1992), 5.
7. Ibid., 13.
8. Hill, 61.
9. Ibid., 61–62.
10. Ibid., 62.
11. Trask, 41.
12. Hill, 63.
13. Boyer and Nissenbaum, 594.
14. Trask, 55
15. Ibid., 57.
16. Ibid., 58.
17. Hill, 65.
18. Boyer and Nissenbaum, 994.
19. Ibid., 683.
20. Ibid., 659.
21. Ibid., 670.
22. Hill, 199.
23. Ibid., 184
24. Ibid., 195.
25. Ibid., 186.
26. Ibid., 179.
27. Ibid, 71.

28. Boyer and Nissenbaum, 476.
29. Ibid., 491–492.
30. Hill, 100.
31. ed. Kenneth Silverman, *Selected Letters of Cotton Mather*, (Baton Rouge: Louisiana State University Press, 1971), 38.
32. Boyer and Nissenbaum, 491.
33. Ibid.,107.
34. Burr, 223.
35. Boyer and Nissenbaum, 9.
36. Ibid., 185.
37. Burr, 244.
38. Hill, 74.
39. Ibid., 75.
40. Ibid., 76.
41. Ibid.
42. Ibid., 74.
43. Ibid., 77–78.
44. Ibid. 85.
45. Ibid., 204–205.
46. Ibid., 80.
47. Ibid., 91–92.
48. Ibid., 76.
49. Ibid., 76–77.
50. Boyer and Nissenbaum, 289.
51. Hill, 80.
52. Boyer and Nissenbaum, 300.
53. Ibid., 302–303.
54. Ibid., 303–304.
55. Hill, 79.
56. Ibid., 81.
57. Ibid., 79.
58. Ibid., 80.
59. David Levin, ed. *What Happened in Salem*, (New York: Harcourt Brace, 1960), 125–126.
60. Hill, 90.
61. Ibid.
62. Burr, 251.
63. Ibid., 477.
64. Ibid., 244.
65. Hill, 104.
66. Ibid., 104.

67. Marguerite L. Harris, Miles F. Harris, Eleanor V. Spiller, and Mary Carr, John Hale, *A Man Beset by Witches*, (Beverly, MA.: The Hale Family Association and Hale Farm, Beverly Historical Society and Museum, 1992), 109.

68. Charles W. Upham, *Salem Witchcraft*, (Boston: Dover Press, 1867), 476.

69. Ibid., 477.

70. Ibid., 478.

71. Ibid., 481.

72. Ibid., 483.

73. Hill, 107.

74. Ibid., 106.

75. Ibid., 108.

76. Ibid., 107.

77. Ibid., 76.

78. Boyer and Nissenbaum, 185.

79. Hill, 80.

80. Ibid., 74.

81. Boyer and Nissenbaum, 444.

82. Ibid., 475.

83. Ibid., 551.

84. Ibid., 683.

85. Nathaniel Hawthorne, "Alice Doane's Appeal," ed. Newton Arvin, Hawthorne's Short Stories, (New York: Vintage Books, 1946), 351.

86. Ibid., 361–362.

87. Hill, 81.

88. Arvin, 362.

89. Hill, 76.

90. James F. Cooper, Jr. and Kenneth P. Minkema, eds., *The Sermon Notebook of Samuel Parris, 1689–1694*, (Boston: The Colonial Society of Massachusetts, 1993), 39.

91. Ibid., 194.

92. Hill, 108.

93. Boyer and Nissenbaum, 600.

94. Ibid., 595.

95. Ibid., 592–593.

96. Ibid., 95.

97. Ibid., 63.

98. Ibid., 67.

99. Ibid., 578.

INDEX

❖

ACKNOWLEDGMENTS

My warm thanks for all their help and advice to Mary Ann Campbell, Barbara Doucette, David Goss, Marilyn Haley, William T. la Moy, Jim McAllister, Juliet Mofford, Gina Muscardine, Bob Osgood, Rev. Catherine R. Powell, Marilynne K. Roach, Paula Ruta, Richard Trask, and Glenn Uminowicz. My special gratitude goes to Webster and Katie Bull and Liz Nelson of Commonwealth Editions, not only for their invaluable assistance but also for their kindness and hospitality. As ever, Alison d'Amario of the Salem Witch Museum was enormously helpful and a rock of support. And, as ever, Leon Arden read the manuscript in its successive stages and made many insightful suggestions. Needless to say, any mistakes are entirely my own.—Frances Hill